NO LONGER I?

Howard Webber

NO LONGER I?

Howard Webber

Gracednotes Ministries

Gracednotes Ministries
425 East Walnut Street
Ashland, Ohio

No Longer I?

Printed in the United Kingdom

ISBN- 13: 978-1519451804
ISBN- 10: 1519451806

'I have been crucified with Christ;
it is no longer I who live,
but Christ who lives in me...'
Galatians 2:20 RSV

CONTENTS

FOREWORD

How do you live the Christian life? Well, believe it or not, the answer is you don't!

Over one billion people have become Christians in the last 2,000 years. But only one person has ever lived the Christian life, and that is Jesus Christ. I am going to make an amazing statement, but I believe it is true. The average Christian knows far more about how to become a Christian than how to be one.

Galatians 2:20 is probably the most comprehensive, compact, complete description of the Christian life in the Bible, 'I have been crucified with Christ; it is no longer I who live, but Christ lives in me; and the life which I now live in the flesh I live by faith in the Son of God, who loved me and gave Himself for me.'

The truth of this verse is simple: Live and let die. Two people have to die in order for you to become a Christian. Jesus had to die for you, but then you have to die to you. Dying to self goes against the grain of human nature, human ambition, and human desire.

The first step to becoming a Christian is accepting Jesus' death for you. The first step to being a Christian is experiencing your death to yourself. You see, the Christian life is a crucified life which then becomes a conquering life.

A.W. Tozer, a great Bible teacher of another generation, put it this way: "A real Christian is an odd number anyway. He feels supreme love for One whom he has never seen; talks familiarly every-day to Someone he cannot see, expects to go to heaven on the virtue of Another, empties himself in order to be full, admits he is wrong so he can be declared right, goes down in order to get up, is strongest when he is weakest, richest when he is poorest, and happiest when he feels the worst. He dies so he can live, forsakes in order to have, gives away so he can keep, sees the invisible, hears the inaudible, and knows that which passes knowledge."

The Christian life is not you living for Jesus; it is Jesus living in you. Martin Luther once said, "When someone knocks at the door of my heart, I open it and they say, 'Who lives here?' I answer, 'Jesus Christ lives here.' Inevitably they will say, 'I thought Martin Luther lived here,' to which I say, 'Martin Luther used to live here, but he died. Jesus Christ lives here now.'"

In October 2012, I received a copy of Howard Webber's book, *Meeting Jesus,* as a gift from General Linda Bond(R). Howard's straightforward and real life stories of the challenges of evangelism inspired me. I shared a copy with the principal of the training college and we agreed that every cadet would receive a copy.

In my opinion Howard has done it again. He has written a candid and straightforward description of the struggles of a follower of Jesus midst the difficulties of life and Christian service.

Read this book with a spirit of joy. Be in prayer. You will discern wisdom, uncover resources and see insights in dying to self and living for Jesus. Your life will be deepened.

Commissioner David Jeffrey
The National Commander of
The Salvation Army
USA

ACKNOWLEDGEMENTS

I would like to express my gratitude to all the people who have encouraged me in my writing, particularly those editors of Salvation Army periodicals who were so kind to me in the early days.

Thank you too to those whose stories are recorded in this book who checked, corrected and verified what I have written.

I am indebted to the late Roy Hession and his book, 'Not I, but Christ,' for opening the gates to what he called a 'preacher's paradise,' and much that I have shared here.

Finally, I am indebted to JoAnn Shade (Major) for her generosity of spirit and time and labour spent in editing and guiding this book to publication. A heart-felt thank you.

PREFACE

Many Christians, having found Christ and known that initial joy that accompanied the discovery, find themselves adrift, perplexed by unexpected experiences and a lack of the abundant life that Jesus promised. It can seem as though there is something missing, something that eludes us. We feel that perhaps if we tried harder and made more effort to become like Jesus, we would find the key to the spiritual success we are looking for: that it is about our achievement, our accomplishment. Yet, despite our best efforts, fervent prayer, and the sincerity of our desires, we are confronted with failure and disappointment time and again.

Like my first book, *Meeting Jesus*, this is a book of two parts. The first part consists predominantly of stories recording various experiences in corps(church) life, my own personal struggle in those situations, and the eventual discovery of the answer. The second part looks at that discovery and the issues that arose in the first part in the light of scripture. My hope in writing this book is that the reader will identify with the ups and downs and the joys and sorrows that I share and, should you be seeking the key to the abundant life Jesus promised, you will be aided in your own journey of faith. God bless you all.

Howard Webber

Fill me with your Spirit, Lord,
Fill me with your love.
Fill this empty heart of mine,
Come down gentle dove.
You see all my self- concern,
Lovelessness and pride;
Help me open up my heart,
Place your love inside.

Fill me with your Spirit ,Lord,
Fill me with your power.
Give to me your source of strength,
From this very hour.
You have seen me trying hard,
Failing every time,
Show me how to let you now,
Live your life in mine.

Fill me with your Spirit, Lord,
Fill me with your joy.
Give to me that happiness
Nothing can destroy.
Even when my sufferings
Point me to despair,
May I know that joy inside
Just because you're there.

Fill me with your Spirit, Lord,
Fill me with your peace,
Quieten all the turbulence,
Bid my struggles cease.
Often my anxieties,
Fill my life with stress,
Show me how to let them go,
Give to me your rest.

PART ONE

THE WOUND THAT WOULD NOT HEAL

CHAPTER 1

A BOLT OUT OF THE BLUE

'I have something I need to say before you go,' Miss Barrett called out as I closed the lounge door, so I opened it again and stepped back into the room. Following a brief preamble she got to the point of why she had called me back, 'I need to tell you that you are the worst officer (minister) this corps (church) has ever had!'

I felt as though I had been hit by a brick and stood there stunned, not knowing how to react to what I had heard. What she said came as such a shock, totally unexpectedly. After a moment's hesitation, I meekly thanked her, (don't ask me why?) and stepped back into the hallway. Letting myself out and shutting the door behind me, I walked down the garden path to my car in a daze. 'Had I heard right? Not one of the worst amongst lesser mortals, but *the* worst, the very least of the least, lowest of the low. How could she have come to that conclusion?' I got into my car, closed the door and put my key into the ignition, but I was unable to turn it, start the engine and drive away, for I could not restrain the tears welling up inside me. The dam burst and I broke down and wept like a baby, inconsolably, like I hadn't wept for many a long year.

When first my wife and I arrived in this North Wales village, to take charge of what was our first corps following training, we commenced visiting and getting to know everyone recorded on our rolls. Dear Miss Barrett was well into her eighties. She had very poor sight and this, together with her walking difficulties and the distance from her home to our hall, prevented her from venturing out to worship. She had outlived her peer group and gradually, over many years, her name had ascended to the top of our soldiers' (members') roll; she was our number one!

When we called on her she was delighted to see us and welcomed us into the area. Subsequently, knowing this dear old soul rarely got out of the house and did not have any close family, when I was passing by I called in to see her. It was no big effort on my part as she lived just off the main road between our village and the nearest town ten miles away.

Miss Barrett was always kind and courteous, insisting on making me tea served from a silver teapot into bone china cups, accompanied by a plate of chocolate biscuits. Concerned at her poor sight and frailty, I would offer to make the tea for her or at least carry the tray from the kitchen to the lounge, but she was emphatic, insistent that she was quite capable of doing it herself. So I would watch attentively, ready to jump to her aid as she came through the door and gingerly made her way across the lounge towards me, before bending down and placing her burden on the coffee table between our chairs.

This became the regular pattern whenever I visited her on my own or with my wife during those first two years. Then she changed. The first thing I noticed was the absence of her cheery, 'Shall I put the kettle on Lieutenant[1]?' when I entered her home, as her warmth towards us was replaced by a cold indifference. Gone too was the natural flow of conversation. Something of a scowl seemed to permanently replace her smile. At first I thought she had had bad news

---

[1]   Lieutenant is a probationary title/rank given to newly commissioned Salvation Army Officers, which they have for their first five years of ministry.

4

or something had happened to her that I had not been told about. When I asked her if she was all right her reply was, 'Yes, why shouldn't I be?'

There was a decisive moment when her mood changed, and I knew that something had happened to upset her, but she would not open up and tell me what it was. It never occurred to me that it had anything to do with me, as I only saw her when I visited her. The only other contact I had with her was by phone when I would ring her to check that she was keeping well. Initially, I thought it was a temporary thing and that things would be back to normal the next time I visited. They weren't. In fact, they were never the same again. A definite feeling began to grow within me that I had said something or done something to upset her, though I had no idea what on earth it could be.

Whilst the visits were no longer pleasant and I no longer looked forward to them, I continued to call there every few weeks just the same. Often I would ask her, 'Have I said anything to upset you? Have I done anything?' to which her reply was always the same, 'No, what could you have said or done to upset me?' I tried apologising for whatever it was that I may have been responsible for, but this was just met with silence. Though I now dreaded these visits, I still felt sorry for this lonely old soul, but I also wondered what good my visits were doing her. They were definitely not doing me any good! Sitting with her in her lounge as she looked out of the window, refusing to say much, placed me in an uncomfortable spot for sure.

About a year after this awkwardness began, I was making my final visit before being moved to a new appointment[2]. I told her what was happening and where we were going, but she showed no interest. I asked her questions about herself and got minimal replies. At the

---

[2]   In The Salvation Army officers do not choose where they go or apply for posts or positions, but are appointed to what is considered by senior leaders to be where God would have them be. These days, in addition to prayer, such decisions are not made without consulting the officer and considering their personal circumstances as well their particular gifting.

end of my ordeal, I prayed with her and for her. As I stretched out my hand to shake hers, thanking her for her kindness to me, (for she had been kind during those first two years), she responded by flopping her limp hand into mine like a piece of mackerel, without holding or gripping my hand in response.

'Obviously, I won't be seeing you again, but I do wish you well and God's blessing upon you. I'll see myself out.' It was as I was closing the lounge door behind me that she suddenly called me back into the room.

'Lieutenant, I have something I need to say before you go.'

In my naivety I thought to myself, 'Thank goodness for that,' as I stepped back into the room, 'this is no way for two Christians to part,' and I then just stood and waited for her to gather her thoughts before she continued.

'As you know, my parents were among the group of pioneers who walked all the way from Wrexham to the village to start The Salvation Army there.' She had told me this several times since first I met her. In fact I learnt much from her about the corps' history. 'And so between my parents and I,' she continued, 'we have known every officer that has ever been stationed here.' That was true, and in the early years officers never stayed more than one year. Many only stayed a few months. In fact, the previous year had been the corps' centenary year and I had researched the corps' history and found that there had been an unbelievable ninety-two officers or officer couples before my wife and I were appointed. I had no idea where all this was leading or the brick of a statement that she was about to unleash on my unprepared ears, something that would fly around inside my head like an unstoppable squash ball bouncing between the walls of a squash court. 'I need to tell you that you are the worst officer this corps has ever had!'

It was quite some time before I was able to compose myself to make my way home. I was relieved that no-one came near my car to observe me while I sat there booing. Several times during that journey home I stopped to check in my mirror to see if the redness of my eyes and all signs of my tears were gone, as my wife had enough on her plate without having to be concerned about me. The children greeted me as I opened the front door, and much noise and chatter followed, but other than Judy commenting on the fact that I was a little subdued, nothing else was said.

We were without a corps secretary so each week I assisted the treasurer in completing the corps accounts and preparing the banking. We did this in the front room of our home. The hall was some distance away and would have needed to be heated before we got there so it was convenient for us both. As we sat opposite one another with the cash and cheques and books between us, the treasurer asked me, 'Is everything all right Leff?' Initially I assured him that everything was all right, but I was quieter than normal and he persisted in his concern for me.

He was a reliable leader and much respected, just a few years older than myself. I knew that I could confide in him. Other than bringing it to the Lord, I had not wanted to share what had been said with anyone else, but I conceded to his persistence. When I finished conveying the story of my relationship over the past twelve months and its culmination, he smiled, 'Leff, ignore her. What does she know about you and what you have done? I know it's not her fault, but she never ever gets to the hall. She's unable to come near the corps. All she knows is what she picks up from the phone calls she gets, and we all know who it is that rings round and upsets folks with their distortion of the facts. Forget it.'

I wanted to forget it. The treasurer was right. What did she know about me or the corps? But I couldn't get it out of my mind. In the days, and indeed weeks and months, that followed I went over and over the last three years of our stay there with a fine tooth comb, analysing, comparing, justifying, and putting together a defence of myself as though I was going to court. 'How could anyone think, let alone say, that I am *the* worst officer they have ever had?'

CHAPTER 2

BEGINNINGS

When The Salvation Army arrived in the village back in 1883, following a ten mile walk by a contingent from Wrexham, crowds flocked into the market hall to find out what all the commotion was about. Just two weeks later in one meeting fifty-one people sought Jesus Christ as their Saviour.[3] A further two weeks and the Wrexham Advertiser reported how some of the worst characters in the village had joined their ranks and that one of the publicans had offered the Army £10 to leave the village as he had only taken half a penny at his public house the previous Saturday.[4]

Following that initial meeting, the Army rented a place from the local butcher where they could meet and worship. The butcher then became the target of the growing hostility on the part of the local publicans whose trade had been so severely hit by what God had done in the hearts of many of their former customers. The publicans boycotted the butcher and encouraged others to do likewise, declaring that they would never give this individual another order 'as long

---

[3]   War Cry November 28th 1883
[4]   Wrexham Advertiser Friday 14th December 1883

as his head keeps warm.' A month later one thousand people sat down for a corps tea and the membership of this new church numbered two hundred and fifty![5]

My wife and I and our two children first drove into the village about 5 pm one Thursday, parking our car outside the council house that was to be our home. A small van driven by another newly commissioned officer had followed us all the way from the training college in London with all our worldly goods aboard. We unloaded it and our friend left with his wife and the rest of the load, all that he and his wife possessed, for their new home some miles further on. Our next door neighbour, a Salvationist, had prepared a meal for us which we were so glad to see. We were very tired and hungry and were to be at the hall for our welcome meeting at 7.30pm.

By the time we finished eating there was no time to unpack, never mind to have a proper look around the house and garden. We all jumped in the car and made our way up the steep and winding road to the main street that ran through the village. It was obvious to any visitor that the village had known better times. Many shops were boarded up whilst others looked neglected and in need of a coat of paint or a complete refurbishment.

We found the worship hall some distance beyond the main street, quite isolated, with a huge length of corrugated iron fencing stretching as far the eye could see on one side, continuing round the back of the hall and beyond on the other. I soon discovered that the fence enclosed a chemical works owned by a giant American corporation. The first thing we noticed as we got out of the car was the pungent smell coming from it! Entering the building we were greeted warmly by those people who had already arrived, but as 7.30 pm drew closer there seemed to be a lack of readiness for the commencement of the meeting. I asked the bandmaster whether I had got the time right?

'Yes, you have, but we can't start yet. Two of my key men

---

[5]   Wrexham Advertiser Friday 4th January 1884

aren't here. They are playing bowls tonight. It must have ended late,' he replied. I kept my thoughts to myself as we waited a further twenty minutes.

'We won! We won!' The shouts startled me and I looked round to see the two jubilant brothers walking down the aisle, waving their arms in the air. There followed a brief résumé of the match before they collected their instruments from the band room and everyone in the band took their places in front of the platform. There were about forty people gathered that evening. Following the meeting, various people came and introduced themselves and several chatted about the corps and the village. I asked a couple of them what the awful smell was.

'That's nothing to what it used to be like. For most of my life it was far, far worse,' said Bob.

'Yes, back then there used to be great white flakes that the works spewed out. They would descend on us like snow,' laughed Walter. 'You would walk up the street and everyone's eyes would be watering,' he added. His words were followed by several of the men doing hilarious impressions of people greeting each other with tears running down their faces.

'Didn't anyone complain?' I asked.

'No, everyone was used to it. No Health and Safety in those days. The owners didn't care about their employees then. They didn't live here. People didn't complain. They were grateful for the work the works provided. They wouldn't have wanted the place to have been shut down,' piped in another man.

'Surely, breathing that stuff, whatever it was, didn't do one's lungs any good?' I said.

'Didn't do our roof any good!' someone muttered, as everyone fell about in fits of laughter. I didn't get the joke.

'What do you mean?' I asked.

'Well, that stuff rots the nails holding the roof slates in place. Every few years we have to replace the rotten nails,' Ivor explained.

11

'Wow!'

'Yes, and it's not good for brass instruments either! We have to keep cleaning them more regularly than we otherwise would because that stuff tarnishes them. In fact the works have been very good to us; they give us a grant each year to cover the cost of regularly re-nailing the slates like we have to, and to compensate for the tarnishing of the instruments.'

As we left the hall to get into the car, I looked at the sparseness of the dwellings that were strewn across the hill facing the front of the hall and wondered why the hall had been built where it had. I later discovered that the hall had not always been so isolated. At one time the hill had been covered with houses; in fact it was a very heavily populated hill. When children grew up, they would often build their homes right up against the homes of their parents. But with the expansion of the chemical works over the previous century and the building of the large council housing estate in the valley sixty years ago, the community on the hill had declined in number. Some of the houses there were not built to a high standard and had fallen derelict, and many had been demolished. All this had left the hall somewhat isolated and quite some distance from where most of the people now lived.

Thus began my education. The village was set in the most beautiful valley, with amazing views when looking out from it. There were so many country walks, a fast moving river with a canal carried across it by a one hundred foot high aqueduct that the world famous engineer Thomas Telford had built. In contrast the village itself was a place of much deprivation and unemployment.

The house we lived in was not only our home but very much a social centre for the estate too. We were not there long before a young unemployed man came to our door asking us for money to tie him over until he received his unemployment benefit. He claimed he had no food in the house and had a wife and six children. I went round and visited him and saw it all for myself. My wife and I then provided him with some food as well as some clothing for the children from clothes we had been given. We also gave him £20 to help him reach his benefit day, together with strict instructions that he was to pay us back when he received it. He could not thank us enough and promised that the moment he got his money he would be at our door to return what he owed. It would be the first thing he did. He allowed us to pray for him and his family before we left. Benefit day arrived, but there was no knock on our door. Nor did he come, as he promised, on any other day of the week that followed.

It was three weeks later that there was a knock at the door and there stood Dougie, looking very forlorn and somewhat embarrassed.

'I'm so sorry Captain,' (I wasn't a captain but that is neither here nor there), 'I meant to come back but I got waylaid and, with one thing and another, the time flew and I forgot, and now I am out of money and out of food. I don't know what to do and it'll be three days before I get my money. Can you help?'

I took him inside and made him a cup of coffee, then said, 'I'll tell you what I'll do Dougie. I will give you another £20 OK?'

'Oh, thank you Captain,' he quickly interjected.

'Hang on a minute, hang on a minute, I haven't finished yet. If you don't bring it back the moment you get your money, don't ever come knocking at my door again because I won't help you, OK?'

'I won't let you down Captain, I promise, I promise,' he replied.

'Don't promise, just do it,' I responded with a smile, and he left our house clutching his £20 note and thanking me for the coffee.

'That sounded a bit harsh,' my wife said after I had shut the door.

'I know, I know,' I replied, deep in thought.

At about 10 am on Thursday morning I opened the door in response to an enthusiastic hard knock only to see Dougie standing there clutching a crisp new £20 note, and beaming from ear to ear.

'There we are Captain, like I promised!' he said in a victorious tone as though announcing he had scored his side's winning goal.

I felt like saying, 'You keep it,' but I didn't. 'Brilliant Dougie! I'm proud of you, well done,' I said as I took the note from him. 'Now make your money last. The benefit should be enough if you don't go and spend it on something unnecessary or silly. It could stretch a lot further if you didn't spend any of it on cigarettes,' I added.

'I don't buy cigarettes, I buy baccie[6] and rizlas[7] and roll my own. That saves money,' he replied. I said nothing further on the subject. I just felt sorry for the lad. He had enough on his plate without lectures from me on the pros and cons of smoking.

Monday morning I responded to a knock at the door. I should have guessed, it was Dougie, bless him. He didn't need to tell me why he had come but he did and I handed him a £20 note. Thursday came and he handed one back to me. This became a pattern. In fact we just put the £20 note under the clock on the mantelpiece above the fire. To us it became Dougie's money.

We would occasionally visit him and his wife and family. He was a bit of a Jack-the-lad character, a loveable rogue. Whenever we were given good clothing for adults or children we would take round what we knew would be suitable and acceptable for him or his family. They were pleased to have us pray for them and their family but they never came near our worship hall, and despite sharing the Good News of Jesus they never made a decision to follow him or receive him as Saviour and Lord . . . well, not while we were there. This is but one example of both the need in that village and the new world we found ourselves in whilst living on that estate.

Things were gradually improving at the corps. Two people who were regularly attending worship when we arrived at the corps, but did not know Jesus personally, sought him and found him as

---

6   baccie – slang for tobacco
7   rizlas are cigarette papers sold in the UK.

their Saviour, Lord and friend. However, despite the many signs of God at work we were not without problems, and not without a lot of prayer being offered as we sought how best to tackle those problems, some of which were of a very physical and very practical nature.

We had a good sized garden shed, but it was somewhat dilapidated. It had been standing in its place for decades and over time it had gradually been sinking into the mud, despite having had its base placed on two thick railway sleepers. Consequently, the floor had been rotting for some time and the damp had been seeping up its sides. The lower six to eight inches of wood was rotten. Also, much of the roofing felt had gone, as had some of the pieces of wood that it once covered. The back garden was a mess, totally neglected and almost waste deep in weeds. In fact, 'wading' through those weeds we discovered all sorts of discarded items including an old rusting car bonnet!

As our two children's bicycles were getting wet every time it rained and they would obviously soon be showing the tell-tale signs of rust, I knew I had to do something. The corps was short of money otherwise I would have replaced the shed with a new one. In the circumstances there was no choice other than to try and salvage what we had and refurbish it. So, with no experience and little idea of how I would do it, I decided I would try and dismantle the shed, lay a concrete base, replace the rotten flooring and cut twelve inches off the bottom of the sides before putting it all together again. I would then need to replace some of the missing timbers in the roof before sealing the whole job from the elements with brand new roofing felt. I am not a carpenter and had never disassembled or assembled a shed before, but what else could I do other than try? Beg your pardon, pray and try?

The corps treasurer was walking his Great Dane along our street the following Saturday morning and, as he passed our house he could hear knocking and banging coming from the rear of it and was intrigued to find out what was going on. Making his way round to the back garden he discovered me trying to dislodge the shed roof. I didn't realise he and his dog were both standing there, watching me, until I stopped to take a breather. Russell suddenly spoke and startled me.

'What are you doing Leff?' he asked, with a bemused smile across his face. I thought I detected the same look on the face of his dog as it gazed at me with its head turned on one side. So I explained to him what I *thought* I was doing.

'Do you really think you can do that?' he asked in response to my explanation.

'I don't know, but I'm going to have a jolly good try,' I answered.

'Would you like me to help you?'

'Would I like you to help me?' I responded, 'That would be really marvellous! Are you sure?'

'I wouldn't offer if I didn't mean it. Let me take Bruno back home and get my tools. You put the kettle on and I'll be back as soon as I can,' he responded, and off he went.

Russell had a senior post in the local authority. Having only recently arrived in the village I didn't know that he had started out as a carpenter, and was a much skilled one at that. In fact he had built his own home, a large imposing house on a hill in the next village. He was the ideal man for rescuing me! I thought he was going to be my aide, but no sooner did he return than he took control and I became *his* helper. I don't think I could ever have completed what I set out to do without him taking the helm.

It's a bit like my journey with Jesus. Sometimes I have felt compelled to do something that I am not skilled at or capable of, and then discovered how God provides for our needs when we are obedient to him. I've heard of Christians refusing to do what they do not feel God has gifted them for, whilst everything that I read in the Bible tells me that we should be obedient whatever we feel about our capabilities or the possibility of succeeding. 'Trust in the Lord with all your heart and lean not on your own understanding,' Proverbs 3:5 tells us. God would have us use our gifts, our abilities and understanding. He gave them all for us to use, but where there is conflict or a contradiction between them and God's word, God would have us obey his word and lean on him not them. Easier said than done.

It took a number of Saturdays to dismantle the shed, clear the area, and lay the concrete, before we were ready to re-erect the shed and re-felt the roof, but Russell did a brilliant job. And although the restored shed was now a foot shorter than it was previously, (and one had to duck when entering the door), it was a perfect shelter for the bicycles and the garden tools.

Looking then to the garden, I wondered whether it had been a film set for the Battle of the Somme! Before it could be levelled for the children to play and ride their bikes in safety, rubbish and weeds needed to be cleared out. Once all the discarded bric-a-brac was removed and taken to the council rubbish tip, and the weeds were cut down, we invited the older members of the Sunday school to come and help shift soil to make most of it level with the path. We provided them with food and fizzy drinks and they worked hard and had much fun. It was a hive of activity and laughter, and they discovered muscles they never knew they had.

Following their help, there was still much to do to prepare it before we were able to sow the seed for the new lawn. Again, there wasn't the money to turf it, which would have obviously given us far quicker results. Eventually however, all was complete. All we needed to do was wait and water, although living in Wales we did not need to do much of the latter. If all went well, by the next summer the children would be able to enjoy it.

As I stood by the fence admiring the finished work, Brenda, the Salvationist who lived next door, came out and sauntered across to me on the other side of the fence.

'I hope you don't mind me saying Leff, but don't you think that all of this is something of a waste of time?' she asked.

'How do you mean?' I replied.

'Well, all this hard work. You'll not be able to enjoy it until next year and then they will probably move you. Nearly every officer that we've had has been moved within two years. Not only that, but most of your predecessors didn't do much with the front garden, never mind the back. Whoever comes might not look after it or appreciate what you have done. Don't get me wrong,' she added, 'I think it will look lovely when the seedlings come through, and being next to our garden I'm so glad all those weeds are gone, blowing all their seeds over to us.' We both laughed, 'But don't you think it a bit of a waste of time and energy? I bet if you come back in a few years time you will see it back to how it was.'

It's the sort of encouragement we all need! But as I thought about it I realised that there was something about the outworking of holiness in it all. Our own personal benefit is no longer the central premise of our lives once we commit our lives to Christ. We live to glorify God and to bless others. Whether or not my family and I would benefit, whether or not I enjoy doing it or not, I should be doing what I am doing for the blessing and benefit of those around me. I should be serving God and my fellow man. I should be serving our successors, God's servants as though I was doing it for Jesus himself, even though I might have no idea as to who our successors might be. They might not know or appreciate all that my wife and I have done. They might not take care of what we leave them. They may even damage or destroy it, but that does not take away our responsibility for doing it. It was a thought I would return to many times in the future.

CHAPTER 3

A PARTICULAR PROBLEM

We spent much time visiting the people and getting to know them, and found them to be good people, supportive and hard working. The corps was not self-supporting financially and required a subsidy from headquarters to cover all the expenditure. However, as people grew spiritually their sense of responsibility increased. Personal giving improved and one small group of ladies brought in extra funds by additional money-raising activities.

In preparing for the corps anniversary weekend that would take place in a few weeks time, we had a meeting where it was agreed that on the Saturday we would have a meal, and those attending would be encouraged to bring some food to share with others. The meal would then be followed by a celebratory festival of praise. We decided not to stipulate what food each person was to bring so that what was eventually placed on the tables on the day would be a surprise for everyone, a faith meal if you like. Having sorted out all the detail for the Saturday as well as the Sunday's worship meetings, we closed in prayer and started to leave the hall. Three ladies were hovering near the front door as I approached to leave and lock up.

'You'll have to ask the bandmaster for the key,' one lady said.

'What?' I said, 'What key?'

'The key to the crockery cupboard at the top of the basement stairs,' she replied.

'Why does the bandmaster have the key to the crockery cupboard?' I asked somewhat confused.

'They are all his and his wife's crocks,' was the joint chorus of the ladies as they laughed.

'I don't understand,' I responded.

'They're on permanent loan to the corps,' one of them added, 'they have been for years.'

'You mean that they want them back?' I asked.

'I doubt it,' she added as all three laughed again. There seemed to be a private joke that I wasn't party to.

'How strange,' I thought as I made my way down the steep footpath towards home. The path was more direct than the circuitous route of the road and consequently it was quicker on foot than by car.

'May I have the key to the crockery cupboard so that we can get the crocks out next Saturday,' I asked the bandmaster after the Sunday morning meeting some weeks later.

'Tell me what time you want them and I will come and get them out for you,' he replied. He was a man well into his seventies who lived some distance from the hall and he didn't drive. Twice every Sunday he and his wife walked to and from the meetings. It seemed silly to me for him to come to the hall just to unlock a cupboard.

'No need for you to come,' I responded, 'just give me the key and when we have finished and put them all away, I will return it to you,' I suggested.

'No,' he said quite adamantly, 'no-one ever has this key. Tell me when you will be here and I will unlock it for you and help get them out.'

I could see this developing into a really unpleasant row, so I conceded, gave him a time to meet me and we parted. 'That crockery must be something really special,' I said to my wife Judy as we made our way home, 'no way will he let me have the key to it.'

He was unlocking the front door when I arrived at the hall the following Saturday afternoon and just grunted in response to my greeting. I followed him through the building into the back room at the top of the basement stairs in silence. As he unlocked and opened the cupboard doors I was shocked at what I saw. There before me was an assortment of various cups and saucers and plates in less than pristine condition. As I lifted them out I could see few matched and a number were cracked or chipped. I thought to myself, 'I would be ashamed to lend these to anyone. I have been to his home and I know that he and his wife would never entertain having them in the house, never mind using them.' It set me wondering, 'Why on earth were they on permanent loan to the corps?'

'See you later bandmaster,' I said as he left the hall. He didn't reply. It was only a few minutes later that the ladies who had agreed to prepare everything for the tea arrived, bringing much needed warmth and joy with them and lifting my spirits. The hall was an old Victorian building, opened in 1888. The toilets, kitchen and storage area were in the basement at the bottom of a narrow, precarious staircase. Following band practice several evenings earlier, some of the men had struggled up the narrow staircase with the wooden trestles and then the large, thick, heavy boards that were to cover each pair of trestles and so make up tables. How they didn't do themselves a mischief negotiating the treacherous stairs I will never know. But this was the way of things whenever we had a social get together.

I shared my observations and concerns with the Corps treasurer when we completed the weekly accounts the next week, wondering what his thoughts might be regarding replacing the crockery and trestle tables. The bandmaster was his uncle, but he responded sympathetically to my concern, 'They desperately need replacing but we don't have the money to do it.'

'So, if the money came in, you would be happy for us to re-place them?' I asked.

'Oh, without a doubt, definitely,' he replied.

God answered prayer. It wasn't long before we received a donation and I was able to travel to Stoke-on-Trent, not too far away, and buy a large quantity of good quality cups, saucers, small plates, bowls and dinner plates from one of the pottery firms there. They were top quality seconds, but one really had to search to discover any flaw or fault in them. Most seemed perfect. They were beautiful and the pottery firm gave us a huge discount. I praised the Lord most of the journey back home. We also purchased six large aluminum tables with retractable legs. They were much, much lighter and easier to manoeuvre. No more lifting of heavy timber or splinters in fingers. Also Russell, the Corps Treasurer, built storage for it all in the room designated as my office, so there was no more climbing up and down those precarious stairs. Everyone was thrilled when they saw them the next time we had a corps meal, everyone that is, except the bandmaster.

'What do you think of our new crocks and tables bandmas-ter?' I asked.

'Where did you get the money for those? I thought the corps was short of money?' he retorted.

'We are short of money, but the Lord has provided,' I said, to which he responded with a grunt. 'Oh, and while we are on the sub-ject, thank you so much for lending your crockery to the corps for so long. Obviously it's yours and you will be wanting to have it back, so please take it when you are able. I'm happy to help you and can get some boxes for you and bring it all to your home in my car if you want me to? Oh, and when the cupboard is empty I would be grate-ful if you could let me have the key. The cupboard belongs to the corps and we're always short of storage space.'

I could tell that he wasn't very happy. It was a long time before he emptied the cupboard and I received the key, but I patiently waited and said nothing. I was not going to be provoked into a dispute over such trivia. The main issue was that the unworthy crocks and trestles were gone and something far better and more worthy of God's house had replaced them.

There were four local officers (elders) in the corps and three of them were in the same family, the bandmaster, his wife who was the Sunday school leader and their nephew Russell. Other family members had been part of this group but they had died. The bandmaster was the oldest of the four and was seen by many as a sort of father figure. To many people in the village beyond the corps, he and his wife *were* The Salvation Army. I was quietly told when we arrived that we would know if we were accepted by those that mattered(?), when we receive an invitation to tea from the bandmaster and his wife. We never did.

As time went on we realised that many were in fear of the man and would never challenge what he had to say on any matter. He was the corps pianist even though there was a far better and more sensitive player in the corps, but no-one would dare risk upsetting him with the suggestion he relinquish the role. When I heard him playing, I often wondered whether the piano had upset him at some time or refused to play the notes when he had pressed the keys? He appeared to be punishing rather than playing the piano. It must have done something truly terrible for the punishment that he was metering out on it!

When sensitive accompaniment was required for a congregational prayer chorus, or when one would have liked to have had a melody softly playing in the background as a member of the congregation spoke to God on behalf of us all, it was no different. He either lacked a gentle touch entirely, or else chose not to use it. So often when the Holy Spirit did move amongst us in a very powerful way, God's work would be interrupted and worshippers distracted by the noise that came out of the piano. Polite requests before the meeting for a quieter accompaniment to prayer were greeted with agreement, but when that time of quiet reflection and petition arrived we were again treated to what I can only describe as an ear-bashing.

I asked Audrey, a gentle lady who accompanied the songster brigade and, on the very rare occasions when the bandmaster was absent, played so beautifully and sensitively for the congregational singing, if she would be prepared to be the corps pianist?

'Oh, no,' she replied, 'he would never give it up, he wants to do it and I would never want to upset him; it would be more than my life is worth.'

What became very clear as time passed was that even the nonsense regarding the key to the crockery cupboard and the crockery being on permanent loan was to do with a power thing.

Yet, despite the negative atmosphere he created, God was at work. The Lord was responding to our prayers. New people were attending the Sunday meetings, and stayed and made our fellowship their spiritual home. We commenced a group that met for prayer and Bible study one evening a week in our home. There wasn't much room in our little lounge, but several neighbours regularly joined with us in addition to the corps folks who came, and one evening one of them, Janet the Post, a retired post lady[8] who lived around the corner from us, accepted Jesus as her Saviour. Whilst she never joined us in Sunday worship at our hall or became a signed up soldier or adherent of our corps, her changed life was a witness to all. To her the small group that met in our home was her church.

---

[8]   Those readers who don't know Wales will not necessarily know that in areas where a lot of people have such common welsh surnames as Jones or Williams or Roberts, where several people might have the same Christian and surname, they are distinguished in the community by people using their Christian name together with the job they do or did, i.e. Glynn the Barber, Janet the Post etc.

CHAPTER 4

MOUNTAINS AND MOLEHILLS

The bandmaster did have moments of kindness but generally he made life difficult for me. I tried to please and encourage him, to show him my desire to work with him, that I wanted us to be on the same side, but his response to my efforts left me somewhat bewildered.

About a year after our arrival I received a surprise telephone call from a young lady who originated from our corps who was now working for The Salvation Army in Liverpool. She explained to me how a tiny corps there was being closed down and that they had a number of brass instruments that she thought we might be interested in looking at with a view to purchasing. She told me that though some were totally unplayable, two or three were in very good condition, and that not much money would be required for them. She wanted us to have first refusal.

A few days later, when I was in the vicinity of his home, I called on the bandmaster, thinking he would be pleased with the news I brought.

'Not interested,' he grunted.

'Not interested?' I questioned.

'No, we don't need any instruments. We have all the instruments we require and a couple to spare, I'm not interested,' he replied, seemingly annoyed at the question.

I left his home with my tail between my legs, as though I had been severely reprimanded for doing something wrong. He wasn't even pleased that he had been offered them. Consequently, I phoned the young lady, thanked her for her offer and explained that we would not be requiring them. I mistakenly thought that was that.

However, a few weeks later I received a call from the young lady to say that her father and mother had been to visit her, and that her father, who was a close friend of the bandmaster, had asked whether there was a euphonium amongst the instruments the corps was disposing of. When she said that there was and that it was one of the instruments that was in good condition, he told her that our bandmaster would probably like to purchase it for the corps. Furthermore, I discovered that the bandmaster was then shown the euphonium and that it had been purchased by the bandmaster from the band's funds without my knowledge or permission[9]!

I was angry, and prayed hard as to how I was to respond. But as I did so I felt the Lord wanting me to do the one thing I did not want to do….nothing! And to say the one thing I did not want to say….nothing! I felt that God would have me wait….but for what? I had no idea but I waited nonetheless. Nothing happened, nothing was said. Whether or not that euphonium was now being used in the band I had no idea. I had never made it my business to look at every instrument in the band so it would be highly unlikely that I would ever be aware that one of them had been replaced. I don't know about you, but I don't like someone thinking they have got away with something, that they have pulled the wool over my eyes when they

---

[9]   In a Salvation Army corps, any capital purchase by any group requires the officer's permission, and frequently needs to be referred to divisional headquarters for approval too.

haven't. I found it very difficult to let him go on thinking I had no idea of what he had done behind my back.

Six months passed and we were coming up to Christmas and the carolling season. During a very general conversation, the songster leader, a very godly man, mentioned his concern that the songster brigade would sound so much better if the accompaniment was better, but that he realised that money would be a problem. There were thirteen people in the songster brigade, but there was little money in their funds. I saw his point. The Welsh are renowned for their singing, and certainly this small group did nothing to belie that reputation. Their singing was beautiful, and their contribution to worship invaluable, as they sang from their hearts as much as they did from their throats. In contrast, the accompaniment provided was from a small, fold-up, portable organ, well past its 'sell by' date. It was operated by the organist pressing foot pedals that blew air into it to create the sound. As good an accompanist as she was, she was never going to turn this sow's ear into a silk purse, (so to speak).

'Take it to prayer and I'll do the same,' I said as the Songster Leader and I parted.

I woke up in the night a few days later with the issue on my mind when an answer came to me. The bandmaster was not only responsible for band instruments, but for all the corps' musical instruments too, including the piano and the organ. At the conclusion of the Christmas carolling, as well as setting aside money for use in the community and corps, a third portion could also be allocated, (at the discretion of the officer), towards the cost and maintenance of the musical instruments. With the high cost of maintaining and replacing brass instruments, frequently in many a corps it was an allocation that went straight into the band's funds. In most corps it had become an automatic thing.

Having just entered November, with just a few weeks to go before our Christmas carolling season was due to begin, I decided to call on the bandmaster and discuss the matter. I shared with him what the songster leader had said and how I agreed that it would be good to replace the little pedal organ with something better.

'That would be good,' he quickly responded, 'but they don't have the money!'

'No, bandmaster, but what I propose to do is to pay for it by allocating that portion of the Christmas carolling proceeds that has been allocated to the band on previous occasions. I've been looking around and have seen what I think would be the ideal replacement in town. If our carolling proceeds are similar to what we have had the last few years we will be in a position to purchase it,' I said, adding, 'obviously I would like the songster leader, yourself and the other leaders to agree with any such purchase.'

I knew he did not like my proposal. 'What?' he retorted, 'you want to get it with the band's money?' with his voice getting louder.

'No, not with the band's money,' I replied, 'with corps money. Whilst a portion of the carolling money has been allocated to the band in the past, it can also be used for the purchase of other than band instruments. As bandmaster, you are as responsible for the piano and organ as you are for the band instruments. Also, the band doesn't need the money as it isn't in need of any new instruments and there is more than sufficient in the band's funds for any instrument repairs or other contingencies that might arise over the next twelve months.'

'For all you know we might be in desperate need to replace some of the instruments,' he replied indignantly, 'I might be relying on that money to be able to buy them. If we don't get the band's share of the carolling money, how are we to do that?' he interjected.

'But you don't need the money, do you? You don't *need* anything.'

'How do you know that?' he said quite gruffly.

'Because you told me you didn't. I sat here in this chair last May and when I asked you if you were interested in having a look at some instruments that were available at a corps that was closing, your

28

reply was, "Not interested. We don't *need* any instruments. We have all the instruments we require and a couple to spare, I'm not interested."

He then leaned back in his chair in stunned silence just staring at me for what seemed to be ages before dropping a bombshell. 'If I don't take the band out Christmas carolling, there won't be any money!' he then said, grinning from ear to ear, 'and don't think I won't.'

I tried not to show my shock or the anger I could feel surging up inside me in response to what I had just heard. Without the carolling income, so much that we were able to do for the needy in the community would be put at risk. I knew what he was saying was not an idle threat. He meant it. From within my heart I cried out to the Lord the most regular prayer he ever hears from me, 'Help!' Now it was me who was the cause of a long silence.

Gradually, as my heart quieted, I sensed light break into the void of my mind. 'Bandmaster, if after thinking and praying about it, you are convinced that the Holy Spirit does not wish you to take the band out carolling, then you have no choice. Whatever you might otherwise feel, it would be wrong for you to do so; you mustn't,' I said. 'I don't think you would ever make such an important decision without bathing it in prayer. Do whatever it is God wishes you to do. I leave it with you,' I added. I then prayed with him, as I always did, before leaving. He sat in silence as I departed. Walking down the hill towards home, looking at the breathtaking view across the valley to the mountain beyond, I cried out to God to do something new within his heart to change his attitude and outlook.

Several weeks passed and nothing more was said on the subject. I was uncertain as to exactly what was going to happen, but as anxious as I was to know what was or was not being planned I managed to keep myself from bringing up the subject with the bandmaster. Then, on the Sunday before the carolling was due to commence, I received a copy of the Christmas carolling programme from a bandsman given the job of distributing them. Was I relieved? The bandmaster never revisited the subject of the conversation that took place earlier and neither did I.

What followed was a month of hard work, with band members rushing their meals as soon as they got home from work or missing them altogether, so as to bring the message of Christ's coming into the world to people in the street in both our village and the surrounding district. Most band members and their families completed their Christmas shopping well before the carolling season began because of the lack of time to do it once we were into December. In addition, both the band members and their families sacrificed each Saturday so that the band and a faithful group of collectors could travel to some nearby town where there was no Salvation Army corps to play carols to the shoppers. Despite inclement weather, it proved very successful, both financially and spiritually, with some new people joining with us in worship on the Sundays that followed.

Early in January I returned to the nearby town to check if the organ/keyboard that I had seen two months earlier was still in the shop, only to discover that a sale was on and we could afford an even better model than the one I had seen previously. But I needed to take the four corps leaders to see it and ensure that they would be happy with what was to be purchased before I could do anything about it. I was nervous.

When I got home I phoned the other three leaders first before then ringing the bandmaster. I swallowed hard and prayed hard before dialing his number, wondering how he would respond as I did so. I told him the other three leaders were able to go to town with me on Saturday morning and I would be picking them up in my car at around nine o'clock. I wanted him to help decide on the purchase too. Would he come? Could he come? If so I would collect him. I waited for his response. For a minute or two I thought I had been cut off, but then he replied in the affirmative. Phew!

Conversation ceased once the bandmaster was in the car. We

arrived at the store and were given a demonstration by the shop assistant. As both the bandmaster and the songster leader could play, they were able to test its capabilities. When they had finished I explained to the salesman that we would need to discuss it and I would ring and confirm one way or the other on Monday.

'You need to know sir,' said the salesman, 'that this is the last one we have and we won't be getting any more.'

'Have you got the corps cheque book, Russell?' the bandmaster asked his nephew.

'No, I didn't think we would need it,' he replied.

'Is everyone agreed that we want it?' the bandmaster asked us all. With everyone agreeing with the purchase, he opened his wallet, asking the salesman what deposit he required to secure it. He counted out the £50 the man requested. I could not believe what I was witnessing and I could see by their faces that neither could the others.

'Here's the receipt, Russell,' the bandmaster said, passing it to him from the salesman, 'don't forget the corps owes it to me.' There had been tension and silence in the car journey to the town, now the relief was palpable. 'Would you all like a cup of coffee,' the bandmaster now asked us. We did not need asking twice. As I sat in the store's cafeteria drinking my coffee, listening to the conversation and laughter of the others, I couldn't help wondering whether it was all a dream. I knew that God had done something but, as is usual with me, I could not grasp exactly what was going on. But then again, I really didn't need to know. My heart was just bursting with thanks and praise to him.

The bandmaster was not without virtue. He was a retired poster painter and a good one at that. As a special corps weekend approached he would ask me what it was that I would like him to do in the way of posters outside the hall. Between these special weekends he would ensure that there was something eye-catching on the poster board, something that would grab the attention of any stranger passing the building should they casually look that way. He was good at producing one line challenges such as, 'What on earth are you doing for God's sake?' Also, when the drama yet to be described in chapter seven unfolded, he was very concerned.

The sad thing, the tragic thing even, is that throughout the years, the bandmaster had been exemplary in terms of sheer hard work. He had been the young people's band leader and shown much patience and interest in teaching the youngsters to play brass instruments. At another time, he been the corps' youth club leader, and he had also been responsible for the corps drama group. Also, leading up to the huge corps anniversary and harvest celebrations that were the vogue in the past, he would spend countless hours preparing the hall with stands and displays. I saw the photographs. They were amazing constructions.

I was also told what a good bandmaster he had once been. Obviously all of this was before my time. When my wife and I arrived on the scene he had already been the bandmaster at the corps for almost fifty years. In fact, when the anniversary of his appointment arrived, we commemorated it with a special celebration and thanksgiving meeting, together with a presentation of an album of photographs taken through the years. I presume that something must have happened to change him and his attitude, his spirit. Or was it a gradual thing, a slow drift from focusing on 'being' to 'doing'? We can be so preoccupied and concerned about what we are doing for God that we lose sight of the more important issue of being what God would have us be, on concentrating on what he would have us know.

It was a problem with Martha, (Luke 10:38-42), who thought the most important thing was what she was doing for the Master rather than listening to what he had to say, as her sister Mary was doing. Tasks can distract us from the One that we believe we are performing them for. Not only that, but we can so easily be too busy about service or cumbered, as the Authorized Version describes, by activities that to Jesus are of no real worth, not what he desires. It was the American theologian John Knox who said, 'It is possible to lose one's soul in a programme of highly useful activity.' Useful it might be, necessary in God's eyes, it might not.

I would love to report that my difficulties with the bandmaster eventually ended, but I can't. There were times when a temporary cessation of aggressiveness and unpleasantness occurred, and times when I wondered whether a real change was taking place in him. But despite never losing my optimism, any hopes I may have had of a permanent change of heart were always short-lived. Nevertheless, I never lost hope and I never stopped praying that God would do the impossible, that he would do that which I knew he was capable of doing.

Poor Moses had similar problems with his leaders, so it should not surprise us that there are problems today with those who will not recognise or accept the authority vested in the one given the responsibility for the whole of a church. It wasn't as if Moses was lording it over his people in an arrogant manner. In fact, we are told how 'Moses was a very humble man, more humble than anyone else on the face of the earth' (Numbers 12:3). Yet Korah, having been given very special responsibilities, made life difficult for Moses, even questioning his authority and qualifications to be in charge of the nation, asking Moses and Aaron, 'Why then do you set yourselves up above the Lord's assembly?' (Numbers 16: 3).

Obviously Moses didn't choose to be their leader; he didn't 'set himself up'. God called him. God put him in that position. He wasn't there as a result of wanting it or conspiring to have it. In fact he was very reluctant to have the job in the first place; he didn't feel himself equipped for the task, even persistently arguing with God, trying to talk himself out of it. Only when God got really angry with him did he submit! (Exodus 3–4:17).

Many of us recognise ourselves in the response of Moses to God's call. We feel that God has obviously made a mistake. Our response has often been somewhat different to that of the prophet

33

Isaiah, as recorded in Isaiah 6:8. When God has been nudging us, calling us for some particular task or function, our response has often been its reverse, 'Here am I, send him!'

Whilst Moses never saw himself as worthy of the role God gave him, Korah was blind to the fact. Korah claimed the 'whole community was holy, everyone of them, and the Lord is with them,' (Numbers 16:3). That may well have been true, though all the evidence, including the attitude of Korah and his followers, would indicate otherwise. But that was not the issue.

The issue wasn't whether or not the community was full of holy people close to God and thus Moses should not have been in a position of more importance than anyone else in the community. God had called him and placed him in that position. Whatever Korah and his followers might have claimed, they then proved their lack of holiness and humility by defying Moses and rebelling against him. In so rebelling against God's servant they inadvertently, perhaps, rebelled against God.

I have discovered through the years that the negative experiences I had in that village corps are nothing unusual. There is always someone, sometimes more than one, a family even, who would make life difficult for the leader, even in places where God is seen to be at work in powerful ways. This is likely true for every church in every denomination since New Testament days. Diotrephes, (3 John 9-10), was one such man who St. John had to contend with. Diotrephes wanted to be top dog and to control others, disguising it as zeal for the truth. Even those given the awesome responsibility of leading a church should not desire to control it, but should wish rather to be its servant and to have both their church and themselves humbly under God's control.

On the hill where most of the population of the village had once lived, (as described earlier), two derelict chapels stood not very far apart. An old man told me the intriguing and disturbing story of how the second one was built. A builder who belonged to the older

34

chapel offered the minister a lot of money for the benefit of the chapel. It was money that the chapel could well have done with, but the builder put a condition on his offer, and that was that he be given a particular position in the chapel and be allowed to determine how the money was spent. The minister refused to agree to the builder's proposal so the builder then threatened to leave the chapel and take his wife and family with him.

The man had a lot of influence with a lot of people and yet, despite that and the fact that the loss of the builder's family would be a great loss to the chapel, the minister refused to be blackmailed. The result was that not only did the builder take his money, his wife and family away, but he then bought a piece of land just yards from the chapel he had left and built another chapel, encouraging family and friends to join him there. The name that the builder gave to the chapel never did become the name by which everyone in the village knew it. No, it gained a nickname and everyone in the village knew it by that name - 'Spite Chapel!'

As I listened to the story I wondered to myself, 'What had that to do with Jesus? What did non-believing observers think when they saw what took place there? It was outside observers who gave that chapel its nickname. What did it cause them to think of Christians? What did it cause them to think of Christ?' It was St Paul who said, 'The scripture says, 'Because of you Jews, Gentiles speak evil of God' (Romans 2:24, GNV). I then thought to myself, 'I claim to belong to Jesus. What is the message I give out? How will what others observe of me affect their view of Jesus?'

Sadly, sometimes there are people in the church who are big and loud, domineering and powerful; people who like their own way, people who make other people feel small, fearful. Others tremble when they meet them. They feel like those first spies that entered the Promised Land, grasshoppers compared to giants, (Numbers 13:32-33), giants who seem to cast a dark shadow wherever they go.

On one occasion, when the children were at school and we

35

were having a particularly difficult time, Judy and I decided to escape for an hour or two. There was a mountain not far from our village and so we drove up its steep twisting road to a place with a panoramic view where we often found solace. Amongst all the beauty that lay before us we could see our village with the huge chemical works belching smoke, (or was it steam?), out of a number of its chimneys. As I pondered the sight, it occurred to me how small everything was from where we sat compared to how it all seemed when we were down there. The few people we caught sight of were mere specks. We saw the village in the context of a far bigger landscape. Those few problematic people, and they were few, who loomed so large and daunting when we were down there, now looked so tiny from this vantage point.

Suddenly I felt as though God was saying, 'This, Howard, is where I want to get you. I want to have you see everything from my perspective rather than yours. Nothing is insurmountable. Those things that seem so large and foreboding down there, look very small indeed from where I am. Your mountains are my molehills and they can be your molehills too. Howard, I want you to live up here with me and operate from here. When you pray I want you to come up and meet me on the mountaintop and join me, viewing the issues you meet from where I am. That way you won't be overwhelmed, threats won't frighten you, fear won't overtake you, and you won't be obsessed with the difficulties and obstacles as if they are all that exists in your world. Eventually, I want you to be able to look on your world permanently from this perspective.'

That brief time had a big impact on my prayer life. I often climbed back up that mountain to that experience without leaving the village. I realised that rather than merely throwing up prayers for God to come down and answer, he wanted to lift me up to view things more clearly from his perspective, to grasp that the only true perspective, (of both myself and the world I find myself in), is his perspective.

Perhaps my experience is best summarized in the simple chorus we'd often sing during our service:

Prayer gently lifts me to highest Heaven,
From earth's confusion to Jesus' breast.
My sin and weakness, my doubt and sorrow,
Are lost forever in sweetest rest.
Hal Beckett

CHAPTER 5

RETIRING THE UNWILLING

Stepping into the Sunday school of that corps was like stepping into another world. I wondered whether it was a throwback to previous age. 'Were even Victorian Sunday schools ever so dire?' I wondered.

Much had to do with the Sunday school's leader. She was seventy-six years old, severe, and rather cold in her attitude towards the young people. 'We will not pray until every eye is closed', she would say, sometimes waiting for a full five minutes before she commenced the prayer. As we waited patiently, one after another of the children would take a peep, if only to see who it was that still had their eyes open, wondering why they were having to wait! 'Oh Jimmy, you've opened your eyes. Now we will have to wait even longer until I can see that every eye is closed. I can wait. I have all the time in the world.' Indeed she had!

Then there was the whistle, a football referee's whistle. Never before had I stood so close to a referee's whistle blown so hard. And it was blown frequently during that hour at an ear-piercing fortissimo, to gain attention, to chastise, or to silence the youngsters. Her preparation was virtually non-existent as after that opening prayer she would ask, 'What shall we do today?'

Auntie Vin, as she was known, was frequently absent without notice, which I would be told later were due to headaches, or 'not feeling up to it'. Added to all this was a superior pomposity; a pride which left me feeling a great anger and resentment towards this woman. Under her regime, few were the young people who would venture into our hall on a Sunday afternoon. Most of those who did were made to go by parents who attended the corps. The few new children who occasionally did venture across the threshold rarely returned a second time. Future prospects for the Sunday school were bleak.

Something had to be done. But as I prayed about it and deliberated on it, I realised that the first 'something', was something that needed to be done in me. I couldn't stand the woman. My spirit towards her was wrong, and I knew that whatever I did, I would probably do the wrong thing in the wrong way because I had no love for her. Consequently, I didn't hurry things. I waited and prayed and watched and got to know her better. Gradually, as I did so I developed a great pity and compassion for her, for I discovered from local people what a good leader she had been in the past. As I visited her home, she proudly showed me photographs of yesteryears' dramas, displays and anniversary gatherings, and she spoke of her young people from previous times in such a way that I felt something of her warmth towards them. I came to realise that at one time her role had been a vocation of love. Now, with her growing health problems and frailty, her sense of insecurity was the cause of the 'rough edges' so apparent in her personality.

None of this justified her behaviour, but having this understanding helped me as I sought to love her amid my frustrations and irritations. I had grave doubts about her spiritual state, but was by now as concerned as much for her as I was for the young people. Because I wanted to handle the situation carefully, I discussed the issues surrounding the need to do something with the divisional commander (regional leader).

The circumstances were complicated by the fact that two of the other three local officers I had in the corps were part of her family. One was her husband, the bandmaster, the other her nephew, the treasurer. Doing anything about the situation might well cause a severe reaction from them no matter how I handled it. I also discovered that some of my predecessors had requested she consider retirement, but their requests were rejected and they then suffered a lot of hostility and non-co-operation for the rest of their stay. I felt that if she was unable to see the situation for herself and was unable to come to the conclusion that she ought to retire, requesting that she give it consideration seemed pointless.

So it was that one Monday morning my wife and I visited Auntie Vin and her husband to discuss the situation and the decision we had made. After some preliminary conversation, I shared with her our thoughts and concerns both for her and for the Sunday school. She agreed quite amicably and appreciatively with our observations, but as I spoke I could tell that her husband was not so approving, as evidenced by the rapidly increasing vigour with which he was rocking his rocking chair. He had worked out where the conversation was going and was not a happy bunny!

I then came to the point and shared with her our decision to retire her and the plans we had for her retirement. We proposed that it take place on Mother's Day in eight weeks time when the divisional commander was to conduct the day's worship at the corps. Although she had never been a mother it seemed appropriate, as she had been a spiritual mother to many. I told her how aware I was that such a decision would leave her with mixed emotions that might manifest themselves in feelings of anger, bereavement, or the like, and that I would come back the following Monday (unless requested to come earlier) to listen, or share, or pray with her. After a little while she told me she would let me know her decision, as though I had made a request. However, I said nothing in reply, knowing her husband had clearly heard exactly what I had said. We prayed together and my wife and I left.

The following Sunday, unusually, both she and her husband were absent from morning worship and she didn't turn up to lead the Sunday school in the afternoon either. No-one knew why. I hadn't received a telephone call to let me know that she wouldn't be there. But no sooner had I arrived home from evening worship than the telephone rang. It was the bandmaster telling me that they did not want me to come to their house the following day, as I had promised, because I had so upset his wife on my previous visit. He replaced the receiver and cut me off while I was pleading to speak to his wife.

The following Sunday, both of them were absent from the meetings again. Two days later, the songster leader, (who was the only local officer in the corps that was not a member of the family), telephoned me. He asked me whether I had heard the story going round the village that the bandmaster and his wife were both leaving The Salvation Army and had their commissions ready to post through our letter-box.

Two weeks earlier, when my wife and I walked to their house, we were both conscious of the fact that something like this might happen as a result of our visit. We were now also aware that the repercussions might go a great deal further than anything we might have foreseen; that there might well be other family members and friends following them. Being such a small fellowship, such a series of events could prove disastrous for the corps, jeopardising its survival. My caller wondered what I was going to do about it. I told him how certain I was that what I had done had been the right thing done with the right spirit in the right way and that God had given my wife and I a quiet assurance in spite of my doubts.

'But you might not have a corps left if you don't reverse this,' he added.

'Then so be it,' I replied.

42

Whatever my certainty, I was not without nagging doubts. I wondered what the divisional commander's reaction would be if I presented the hall keys to him because the corps we had been given was no longer there? Would we even be considered for another appointment?

While I was away, some of Auntie Vin's family got together to discuss how they were to deal with me, and I returned to hear all sorts of rumours as to what I was supposed to have said to Auntie Vin and her husband, none of which were true. I was so glad to have taken my wife with me as a witness to what I actually said. Some people judged me to have been wickedly hurtful to such a dear old couple. Resentment and ill-will towards me was not limited to family members or some of the corps. To the small community around the corps, that husband and wife 'were' The Salvation Army and thus whatever I had done must have been wrong.

I had never felt so lonely. Often, in the days and weeks that followed, I would meet the bandmaster in the street and ask after his wife and request that I be allowed to visit her. His reply was always brusque and negative, and always he would say the same thing, 'She does not want to see you. You are not to come to our house.' Nevertheless, I would ask him to convey my concern to her. Meanwhile God blessed me abundantly through their nephew who was the corps treasurer. I did not anticipate Russell's support, especially as he began to bear the brunt of the family's resentment for sticking by me, yet he proved a rock amid the storm as he quietly stood firm and backed me.

During the weeks that followed, I kept Russell and the divisional commander informed of each meeting on the street with the bandmaster. He still did not come near the hall. Over that time people in the corps who had not been happy with me following what had happened, gradually warmed towards me. They also became exasperated with the situation. A couple of soldiers began to speak ill of Auntie Vin and the bandmaster and their stubbornness, as well as their unwillingness to meet and talk with me or attend worship. Imagine their confusion when, in response to some critical comments, I spoke in their defence? They thought they had been supporting me in saying what they did.

On the day before the planned retirement ceremony, I still had no indication of whether Auntie Vin would attend the Sunday evening meeting when her retirement was to take place, though I heard a rumour that she was coming. I happened to see her husband out on an errand that morning and asked him about what I had heard, to which he replied, 'If she does come, it will be nothing to do with you!' In response I told him I would be pleased to see her whatever her reason for coming.

In the afternoon I received a telephone call from divisional headquarters, asking to be brought up to date regarding the situation. When I told the speaker that I was still not too sure whether there would or would not be a retirement ceremony within the meeting, I was told I ought to swallow my pride and visit them. That remark hurt me deeply. I never dreamt that anyone would have considered pride to be the controlling factor in me not visiting them. I had been told categorically not to visit by Auntie Vin's husband. My frequent requests to see the lady had been persistently refused and I just could not see how going against their clearly stated wishes would achieve anything in the long run.

Sunday evening came. The hall (unusually) was packed, and I was standing outside the door when, coming up the road towards me, I saw the bandmaster and his wife. My heart started to beat discernibly within my chest as they approached the building. I offered Auntie Vin my hand in welcome, but it was brushed aside as they passed by, ignoring me. A little while later I entered the hall and began shaking hands with those already seated. When I got to the row in which Auntie Vin and her friends were sitting, whilst they each responded with a handshake she refused the offer of my hand and ignored me.

The meeting began, and when the time arrived for the retirement ceremony she was invited to the platform by the divisional commander and sat in the chair next to me. She was shaking. I tried to reassure her by touching her elbow. This she shrugged off in full view of the congregation. You can imagine my emotions. The divisional commander spoke and then presented her with a certificate recognising her service, together with a host of letters of tribute from previous officers of the corps whom I had managed to contact. She also received a beautiful clock bought with the proceeds of the donations given for her, after which she was given opportunity to respond. As she walked forward to speak I trembled with fear as to what she might say to the assembled crowd, but I need not have worried. She gave the most moving testimony, glorifying God and thanking him for the privilege she had been given to serve him.

At the end of the meeting, as I stood outside shaking hands with those leaving, she came towards me, laden with gifts and greetings. I offered my hand once again. This time she broke down and wept. 'I had no idea that you had arranged all of this for me,' she said.

'When I left you the last time I saw you, my closing words to you were "I love you Auntie Vin". Nothing that has happened since then has altered that. I still love you,' I told her. Her husband just scowled.

The following day, I said to my wife Judy, 'Let's visit the bandmaster and his wife, I know the door is now open and I'm certain that it's the right thing to do.' She agreed. There was a narrow alley between their house and their next door neighbour's property, and as we came out of the alley into their backyard there she was in the sunshine, pegging out washing on her clothes line. On seeing us she gave us a beaming smile and words of welcome. 'Put the kettle on Les, the lieutenants are here.' I looked through the open door and saw her husband in his rocking chair, none too pleased with this request and not at all happy to see me or my wife. However, we had a lovely time of sharing with Auntie Vin as we drank tea together. Her husband had very little to say before we ended our visit with prayer.

Her health improved over the months that followed. Many felt it was because the pressure of responsibility had been removed. But there was one more final illuminating incident to come. Sometime later her nephew Russell, the corps treasurer, came as he usually did to complete the corps' weekly accounts at our house. As we concluded and sat together drinking tea, he told me how, on his way to our house, he had popped in to see how his uncle and aunt were doing. In their conversation his aunt had discussed Judy and I and told him how much she had taken to us. Her only disappointment, she said, was that we had promised that we would visit her the week following our breaking the news that we were going to retire her, but that we had failed to do what we promised.

'But Auntie Vin, whenever lieutenant bumped into Uncle Les he would always ask if he could come and see you, and Uncle Les would always tell him that you did not want to see him; that he wasn't wanted,' Russell had responded.

'Is that right Les?' she had then asked her husband. 'Did you keep telling the lieutenant I didn't want to see him?' Apparently her husband sheepishly refused to answer her. Unbeknown to me, his attempts to hurt me had resulted in him hurting her.

How hard it is to walk with God in the darkness when one cannot see the way clearly or imagine what the eventual outcome might be. But how faithful God is to his promises!

'All of you that honour the Lord and obey the words of his servant, the path you walk may be dark indeed, but trust in the Lord, rely on your God' (Isaiah 50:10, GNB).

CHAPTER 6

DOORS THAT OPENED

I had planned a busy afternoon visiting various members of the corps when I felt a compulsion to go to a large printing company in a nearby town with material I had collated for the corps' centenary brochure. The purpose was to see whether they would be willing to purchase some advertising space. I knew nothing about such things and was learning the ropes as I went along. Some months earlier I had approached the self-same company thinking that they might possibly print a relatively small order free of charge! Yes, I am a dreamer.

On that occasion I never got past the receptionist, so any thought of returning to the company did seem somewhat foolish! Negative thoughts filled my mind. Even though this time I would have something tangible to show them, why would they be any more interested in seeing me than last time? Would I ever get beyond the receptionist and have an opportunity to present my proposal to someone who could make a definite decision?

With mixed emotions and uncertainty, I returned home, collected all my material, and drove the seven or eight miles to the printer. As I entered the company's reception area, I was surprised to see a large pile of brown paper packages, each with an envelope attached with the words *The Salvation Army* printed in bold type, together with the army's logo on them. They were obviously envelopes for our forthcoming nationwide appeal to the general public in support of our work amongst the needy and underprivileged. I had always considered my 'patch' to be a far-flung, forgotten outpost, miles from civilisation and any metropolis! Prior to my assignment there, I had never heard of this printing firm, and wondered how The Salvation Army had become one of its customers. While I was contemplating all of this the receptionist returned and ushered me into the boardroom, introducing me to the managing director. After a few words of introduction, I laid out what I had prepared on the boardroom table and explained what I was trying to do. He seemed genuinely and greatly interested.

'Would you mind if I called in one of my people to look at this?' he asked, when I finished my explanation.

'Not at all,' I replied, and he left the room, returning a few minutes later with another man.

'This is one of my graphic designers,' he said as he introduced his companion. After a few moments conversation in which I tried to explain what I was endeavouring to create, much embarrassed at my meagre, inartistic attempts to design the cover, they stepped aside for a few private words. Turning back to me the MD said that not only would they be willing to purchase a full page of advertising space, but they would both design and print the cover for me free of charge if I would like them to.

'Wow! What an offer,' I thought, and eagerly confirmed my acceptance and gratitude. In addition to thanking them, I suggested that they might like to print their own advert using the inside of the brochure's back cover, (which I had planned to leave blank). They both thought that was a good idea. This meant that I still had the same number of pages available for advertising when I left the building as I had when I went in! As I walked past the huge pile of annual appeal envelopes on my way out I couldn't help wondering why I had been treated so differently this time. Did they think I was a 'somebody' from headquarters in London, rather than the 'nobody' from a village up the road? Who knows? But I felt that the Holy Spirit had led me there and created the whole scenario that afternoon, and I spent the return journey praising and thanking the Lord.

Following the initial refusal of an audience with the managing director of that firm months before, I had sought quotations from other printing firms. From the figures I received I calculated that I would need to charge twice the price that I wanted to, just to break even. I didn't want the brochure to be merely for those who attended our corps. I wanted it to be of interest to the wider community, a way of reaching out to the unchurched people of the village, a vehicle for the gospel. But I knew that the financially deprived folks of the village would not have been willing to pay the full cost.

After much thought and a lot of prayer I decided on a price that was less than half what it would cost us to print, even with the advertising proceeds, a decision that would look foolhardy to even a casual observer. As mentioned previously, our small corps struggled to keep its head above water financially, so I could not afford for the brochure to make a financial loss. Yet, despite the uneconomic price, I felt I still had to keep advertising to a minimum. Thus I decided to limit it to just two pages out of the twenty four. I did not want advertising to appear on every other page and to swamp the brochure.

The next company I approached was the huge chemical works that was behind the fence that went round the back of our hall. As with the first company, I arrived one afternoon with no appointment and, after a short delay, was ushered into the office of the works manager. He offered me far more money than I had decided to charge for a full page advertisement and, in addition, gave me an equal amount from the company's charity fund. I was gobsmacked! (I've discovered that expression is now to be found in the Oxford Dictionary!). He told me that he didn't want the page of advertising space that he had just bought, and to sell it to someone else.

When I asked him why he didn't want to advertise, he replied, 'Do you know what we manufacture here?'

'Aspirin?' I queried.

'Not exactly,' he answered. 'We manufacture salicylates for the pharmaceutical industry. They are the ones that make it into the aspirin tablets you get at the pharmacy. So you see, none of your anticipated readership are ever going to be customers of our company.'

'Well, with so many of your workers living in the village I would like to place something in the brochure to acknowledge your support for us,' I responded.

'That's up to you,' he replied.

This visit appeared to me a complete vindication of my decision to minimise advertising and keep the cost of the brochure uneconomically low. I could hardly restrain my excitement as I thanked the man and made my way to the door. I had two pages of advertising space to sell, had been paid for three, and still had yet to sell the two pages I started with! The amazing thing about that brochure is that by the end of the centenary year, rather than finishing with the deficit we anticipated, we ended with a huge profit!

Now my wife and I had been praying much regarding the fact that our worship hall, though in good condition, was in completely the wrong position in relation to where the majority of the people in the village now lived. We could not think of any good reason why anyone, with no commitment to Jesus, would ever want to venture up the long walk to our hall from the estate in the valley below, even though some new people had joined since we arrived. Yet we didn't possess the finance needed to acquire a site and erect a new building down where the people were, an area both socially and financially deprived. In other words it was not an environment for raising money. Nor could we place our present building on casters and wheel it down the hill!

The definite and obvious need down in the estate for the

gospel and for a community centre was clear to Judy and me. We came to the conclusion that it would need the intervention of God himself in a miraculous way for anything to be done about the situation.

Although we saw it as an impossible conundrum, we were used to the Lord surprising us with answers to prayer, answers that we could never have imagined. What is it God says? 'For my thoughts are not your thoughts, neither are your ways my ways," declares the Lord' (Isaiah 55:8), and again, 'Trust in the Lord with all your heart and *lean not* on your own understanding' (Proverbs 3:5). Yes, God gave us brains and he definitely wants us to use them, but he doesn't want us to place our reliance on them rather than him. Our knowledge and our experience and our understanding are always limited, although that limit varies from person to person. What God can do and often wants to do is frequently more than we could ever have imagined (Ephesians 3:20). Our problem is that we don't expect enough of God. But God never disappoints. Expect little and one will receive little; expect much and one will receive much. Oh, may we be a people who expect much from God.

As I turned the handle of the door to leave the works manager's office, a thought suddenly jumped into my head and I reopened the door. Have you ever started to say something or ask something and no sooner have the first words left your lips than you realise that you need to qualify what you just said? So you tag on another sentence, then realise that that needs to be clarified, and so you add another sentence, then another. Before you know where you are you reach a point where you wish you had never started and are acutely embarrassed. Ever been there?

'Oh, by the way. I know nothing about your works here, and I can't see over the fence, but if ever you have a building here that you don't want,' I hesitated, 'obviously it would have to be portable....oh, and I don't mean an office-type portakabin ... it would have to be something big enough for a small congregation to meet in

51

… and in good condition.'

By now the man was sitting bolt upright in his leather chair looking at me in a very strange way. I wondered what on earth had possessed me to ask the question in the first place. With every attempt to clarify the very simple question I had started out with, I felt myself getting hotter and hotter, wishing I hadn't started. Wishing that a big hole would appear to swallow me up and take me away...'err, and we haven't any money so it would have to be given to us ... free, I would be interested?' I stopped.

There was silence. He just sat in his chair, arms folded, looking back at me as though I had said something really shocking. 'Was he waiting for me to leave?' I wondered. I felt so foolish.

Maybe he was thinking, 'Why didn't you get out while the going was good?'

After what seemed to be an interminable time he asked me a few questions, and then got out of his chair and beckoned me over to the large window that overlooked the works.

'See those two terrapins?' he asked pointing to I knew not what! I was confused. The only terrapins I had ever heard of were those little turtle things I have seen in aquariums or in nature programmes on television. Not only that, but what greeted my eyes at his panoramic window was such a complex of pipes, buildings, chimneys and silo-like constructions that I probably would not have been able to see what he was pointing at, had I known what to look for.

'Come over here,' he then said, leading me to an aerial photograph of the chemical works on the opposite wall. 'See those two buildings?' he asked. To me they looked like tiny matchboxes. 'They are about twenty foot wide by thirty foot long. If you can find a site, get planning permission and transport, they are yours,' he added. I was flabbergasted. I was in such shock that all I could say was, 'Oh, thank you very much.' I left his office overwhelmed at two amazing surprises within minutes of each other. I got into my car thanking and praising God.

I had arranged what I was to do for the rest of the afternoon but I needed to tell someone what had happened, so I quickly drove the mile or more home in the hope that Judy would not have left yet. She had planned to spend her afternoon visiting people. Sure enough she was still at home.

'I thought you were not coming back till teatime,' she said as I entered the kitchen..

'I wasn't, I wasn't, but I needed to catch you before you left,' I said.

'Why?' she asked with her brow furrowed.

'Well you know how we have been praying and praying that God might somehow give us a building down here in the estate?'

'Yes,' she replied.

'Well, you'll never believe it. He's just given us two!'

'Now you're being silly,' she laughed.

'No, I know it sounds ridiculous and far-fetched, but it's true. I was leaving the office of the manager of the chemical works when a thought popped into my head, and I asked him if he happened to have a portable building that he no longer required, and he offered me two!'

'Really?'

'Yes, really! Obviously I haven't seen them yet, but isn't that amazing?'

'That is amazing,' she answered with a look that matched her words.

Together Russell, with his building experience, and I arranged an appointment to see the buildings. They were in good condition and ideal for our purposes. There were some pieces of wood that would need replacing and both buildings would need a lick of paint and some alterations, but we were both amazed at their condition. We promised to return once we had managed to get ourselves organised

Our local councillor had been made deputy mayor of the

nearby town which also covered our area, so I visited him and shared with him all that had happened. He seemed as excited as I was and suggested a site that the council owned and might well allow us to have. It was a piece of waste land where a former coal mine shaft had been capped. Subsequently, he was able to confirm that it was available for us and that he would help us with our planning application. Not many miles away in another village there just happened to be a company that hired out heavy plant machinery such as earth movers and huge transporters. A visit to that company resulted in a promise of free help transporting the buildings to their new site.

Every visit, every conversation was bathed in prayer. We felt that God was leading us in a most remarkable way. Whilst visiting the chemical works' social club with the War Crys one Friday night, a few weeks after my encounter with the works manager, I approached a group of men who sat around a table in deep conversation.

When they looked up at me one of them asked, 'Are you The Salvation Army guy who met with our boss a few weeks ago and asked him if he had a building you could have?'

'Yes, I am,' I answered. My reply was followed by all four men looking at each other and laughing.

'He hasn't got over it,' the man then said.

'Neither have I,' said I.

'No, you don't understand. We have just finished a research project that was housed in those two buildings. That day you visited him, we had had a meeting in the morning where we discussed the fact that we needed to clear the area where they stand to make way for a new brick-built building we have planned for the site. The boss said that it would be such a shame to break up those two terrapin buildings as they were in good usable condition, and asked us if we could come up with any ideas as to what to do with them before our next meeting. We broke up for lunch at 1 o'clock and when the boss returned to his office an hour later, apparently there you were sitting in his reception area waiting to see him. When you asked him if he had a building he did not want, he could not believe his ears. He knew you knew nothing of our meeting and just couldn't get over the timing of your visit!' To me it was yet another confirmation that we were tuned into something God was doing.

The next thing I needed to do was to call a meeting of the corps and present to the people all that had happened, together with possibilities and proposals for the new buildings. Everyone for whom the corps was the spiritual home, not just those who were 'signed-up' members, were invited. Still feeling my way in terms of exactly what God had in mind, I felt that we weren't to presume anything or jump to conclusions that God had not confirmed. Also I had to avoid the vision being dropped out of the sky into their settled lives like a bombshell.

About thirty people turned up that evening. After some prayer and worship, I began by sharing something of the recent history of the corps and its decline, together with my concern that we were not reaching the people of the village very effectively. Having said that, I praised the Lord for the fact that people had come to the Saviour during the previous twenty months. I told them of Judy and my prayers regarding the hall and then what had transpired during my visit to the chemical works. By now we were in the corps' centenary year and the brochure had been printed and was selling well, so I included something of the wonder of what God had done in making it possible to produce such a professional production at so low cost.

Russell, the treasurer, spoke about the condition of the buildings and the work that lay ahead, and I then told them about the piece of land, the support of the deputy mayor and the plant hire company's willingness to help. I then reassured them that we were not leaving our present building and that our morning and evening worship would remain there for the foreseeable future.

What I proposed was that our midweek ladies' meeting, for which my wife was responsible, would relocate down there. The Sunday school, which I was now responsible for, would also move down into one of the buildings, and I proposed that the other build-ing would be a café and shop selling quality second-hand clothing. This would create a much needed centre where people could meet together, and provide good quality clothing at affordable prices for the families who were struggling to make ends meet. The venture would also generate an added income to the corps to support the new venture and any other initiatives we might later feel led to start. More than that, it would also give opportunities to interact with peo-ple in terms of sharing Jesus in both word and deed.

I tried to reassure them that there were no plans at present to move morning and evening worship from our present premises, but what I did propose was that once a month we have an extra after-noon meeting down there in the estate focused on those contacts we would be sure to make.

'After six months we will review the situation. Obviously, if the work down there prospers and more people attend that once-a-month meeting than either meeting up here, I would suggest that God might well be saying something to us, and that we would need to respond,' choosing my words very carefully. I then asked the peo-ple to react to what they had heard.

At first there was a palpable air of excitement in the room as one after another spoke positively about the need of the corps to change and the opportunity that all of this would offer. Others were more guarded and asked questions about what we would then do if it all proved a success. I tried to reassure them that I had no plans, but that if all of this was of God then he would have plans for what we do next, and we would need to seek out from him what those plans were. The response was generally a very positive one, that is, until the bandmaster spoke up. He had been silently listening to all that was being said. I knew that his view would be critical.

'Leave a solid, brick-built building for a prefab? Ridiculous!' he said. I restated that the proposal was not to leave the brick-built hall for a prefab. I begged him to at least take the proposal away and

56

think and pray about it. But my suggestion was met with ungracious remarks and contempt. 'I have been here all my life, *this* is The Salvation Army, and we will *never leave this hall.*'

Those who disagreed with him seemed too timid to voice their opinion any more after that. I knew that it would be an uphill struggle if I didn't have the support of all the corps leaders. We were very small in number and I couldn't do all that needed to be done on my own. I needed the support of all the leaders and without this particular leader that support would never be forthcoming.

I believed it then and believe it still, (all these years later), that the whole of the corps' future and the progress of the gospel in that place hung in the balance. What I had shared was new to everyone except Russell. I knew that they needed time to absorb all that they had heard so, taking up the words I had just heard, I asked them to listen to me very carefully, before I closed in prayer. 'My friends,' I said, 'I need to tell you very clearly that the day will come, one way or the other, when you *will* leave this hall.'

Sadly, the bandmaster would not reconsider, and the corps remained split on whether or not to embrace the proposals. Though unsure of how to resolve the situation, I felt compelled to pursue what I believed God had planned, so over the next few months I had meetings with various bodies, making slow progress until something happened that stopped me in my tracks and was to change everything.

CHAPTER 7

FROM THE MIDST OF A STORM
(Written at the time)

Until recently we were a happy settled family: my wife Judy, Christopher aged nine years, Sarah eight years, Naomi eight months and a little one due in six months time to be a partner to Naomi. Three weeks ago Christopher was a bit poorly, but we were not too concerned. Two weeks ago things were a little bit more serious and our general practitioner referred him to a paediatric consultant at the hospital. Whilst I was at the hospital with Christopher, Judy was informed by phone that her blood screening test for spina bifida had given a positive result.

'Don't worry, your dates are probably wrong,' they said, but we had made a careful and deliberate note of the dates, as the baby was planned. 'Don't worry, the other possibility is twins,' she was told. But there is no trace of twins in either of our families. I came home from hospital to find Judy in floods of tears. I was angry that such a result had been given her over the telephone, yet when I made enquiries the following day, they were met with a denial that any such thing could happen. Asking for a reassurance that my wife had imagined it, and confirmation that the result was not positive, the ante-natal clinic refused to confirm or deny it.

We kept telling ourselves that it couldn't possibly be spina bifida and yet we were not convinced. As that week progressed Christopher entered hospital for observation and more tests. Despite some pain, he did not seem too bad in himself. We brought him home for the weekend but had to take him back again Monday morning for further investigations. The pain he had been suffering increased quite dramatically over the weekend and by now he was having difficulty walking. He cried out loudly with the pain despite my efforts to carry him to the car with as little movement as possible. I stayed with him at the hospital throughout the day.

The following day I returned to the hospital to spend another day with him, at the end of which I went home for some food and to catch up on my work. I hadn't been home very long when we received a telephone call from the hospital, 'The consultant wishes to see one of you in the children's ward at 6.30 pm tonight,' said the sister. I explained that I had been there all day and would be coming in again in the morning.

'The consultant is coming in from home especially. He needs to see you tonight,' the sister then added, with a tone of urgency in her voice.

'You are making it sound very serious,' I said.

'I can't discuss it on the phone,' she replied, so I assured her I would come.

Judy and I both sensed the impending gravity of what was to follow even though we could not imagine what it could be. Knowing the state Judy was already in regarding her own news, I asked Russell and his wife Honor to come and keep Judy company while I went to the hospital.

'I'm afraid that Christopher has leukaemia,' the consultant paediatrician said.

'Leukaemia? My son?' My stomach reacted as though it had

60

been punched, and my head numbed suddenly at the same moment as though it had shared the blow; a numbness that remains.

'Are you sure?'

'Quite sure, though exactly what type of leukaemia has yet to be diagnosed. If it is the most common type then there is a good chance that it might respond to treatment and we might save him.' I left the sister's office bewildered and popped in to the ward see my little lad. He was both pleased and surprised at my unexpected visit at that hour. But I could not stay. I had to leave quickly for I was nearly choking with a grief that cried to be released.

'How am I to tell Judy?' I thought, as tears trickled down my face on my journey home: 'If he has the most likely type of this disease, he has a forty-five per cent chance of recovery,' the consultant had told me.

I had my feelings under control by the end of the ten mile journey home, but as I opened my mouth to speak, Judy's eyes pierced my defences and the words tumbled out with the tears. My normally very quiet wife screamed in response to the news and punched the walls, something totally out of character, something I had never ever seen her do before. Honor, who had been keeping her company, broke down and wept as her husband left the room and went into the kitchen to put the kettle on and probably hide his own feelings.

We were devastated. The following day Christopher had to be taken the fifty miles to Liverpool where there was a specialist oncology unit in the Alder Hey Children's Hospital. The paediatrician had advised me that one of us travel with Christopher in the ambulance. Judy wanted to go, but she also had an appointment at the ante natal clinic. She needed to discover more regarding that terrible phone call she had had the previous week. I phoned officer-friends at the next corps to see if they could drop everything to look after Judy and our other two children, and take her to the clinic as she didn't drive. Judy wanted to be with her little boy but she needed to keep her clinic appointment. I wanted to be there for her, but also be there for our son. The following morning I said good-bye to Judy, Sarah and Naomi and drove to meet up with Christopher at the hospital. Judy felt torn apart . . . I felt torn apart . . . Sarah was confused and Christopher bewildered.

No sooner had we entered the hospital in Liverpool than cerebral spinal fluid, bone marrow and blood were taken from him.

'I confirm that your son does indeed have leukaemia but it is the most common and treatable sort,' the consultant told me a few hours later. 'It will require an intensive regime of treatment and it will probably be three years before we can say that he has fully recovered and there is no sign of leukaemia cells. Even then he will need periodic check-ups. Ninety per cent of children make an initial positive response to treatment and get back home after three months, but of these, fifty per cent recover and the other fifty per cent regress, deteriorate and die in the months that follow.'

'It can't be true, not MY Christopher ... it's not true ... it can't be happening to us!' I had thought that somehow they would discover that a mistake had been made with that initial diagnosis at the other hospital; that the results of the tests at this hospital would prove the other's results wrong.

'How do you want to handle this?' asked the consultant. 'Do you want to tell him or keep it from him?'

'I can't keep it from him. If the worst comes to the worse and he realised that I had kept the truth from him or lied, I would never be able to live with myself.' With the consultant in tow, I popped into the ward and sat on the edge of Christopher's bed.

'What's going to happen, Daddy?' he asked

'Christopher,'

'Yes, Dad.'

'You know that you have been quite poorly?'

'Yes, Dad.'

'Well you have an illness called leukaemia. It is a very serious illness and some children have died from it' (I felt that by phrasing it like this he might think of it as being a long time ago rather than something so recent as to frighten him), 'but this doctor is very clever and is going to do everything he can to make you better, OK?'

'Yes, Dad. That's a lovely name.'

'What is?' I asked quizzically.

'Leukaemia, it sounds like Luke in the Bible,' he replied. Dear Christopher, he could make me smile even at such a critical and up-setting time. I was then called to the phone, it was my officer friend Paul who, with his wife Julie, were looking after the rest of my family.

'Hi Howard, how are things with you?'

'They have just confirmed that it is leukaemia,' I replied.

'I'm so sorry mate,' Paul commiserated, 'are you sitting down?'

'I know, they've confirmed that Judy's expecting a spina bifi-da child.'

'No mate, it's twins … (SILENCE) … are you still there?'

'Paul, I know I have a sense of humour but that isn't funny,' said I, trying to take in what he had just said.

'Mate, I wouldn't joke like that at a time like this.'

I knew that he wouldn't, and even now am not sure quite why I said it, 'I know, I know, sorry,' I said.

'Look I'll put your wife on,' he then said. Judy was so emo-tional, laughing and crying all at the same time. Laughing with relief at the news that she wasn't having a spina bifida child; crying at the news of what Christopher had and the possible prognosis, as well as the thoughts of how we were going to cope with having twins on top of everything!

Following the phone call I returned to Christopher's bedside.

'You have something many other children don't possess.'

'What's that, Dad?'

'You have Jesus in your heart, don't you? You don't just be-lieve in him, you know he's there.'

63

'Yes, Dad, I do.'

We prayed together at his bedside and a kindly officer who discovered I was there took me the fifty miles home.

Back home, Judy and I are stunned. We pray and weep until we are drained of emotion. We cannot hide or bury our sorrow and Sarah weeps too. Christopher needs one of us with him as the treatment is severe, and so next day we part as I return to Liverpool. In the evening I return to tell Judy that a side room on the ward, big enough for a cot for Naomi as well as a single bed for her, has been vacated, and staff have arranged for her to move into it the following day. There is little space, little privacy, but close proximity to the little chap who needs their company. Not only will Christopher have the company of his mummy and his eight month old sister Naomi, who would live up to her name and prove to be a delight to her big brother, but Judy will be compelled to rest as the ante natal clinic ordered her to, something she would never have done at home.

Early the following morning, all four of us travel back to spend the day with Christopher. Then, in the evening, just Sarah and I come home, leaving mummy, Christopher and Naomi behind. The house is quiet and we sit and cuddle up on the settee and weep and pray together, until she is so tired that I carry her upstairs and tuck her into bed. In the silence God speaks:

God is love, I know, I feel,
Jesus lives and loves me still.

Today Sarah returned to school. I travelled again to Liverpool. This is the fifth day. Christopher is very down, 'I wish they would make me sleep forever like at the vet's, Mum.' . . . The battle has only just begun.

In a drawer at home are three dedication certificates. We gave our little ones back to God for him to use as he saw fit. We live for God, we seek his will daily and strive to obey it and so we know that nothing can get through the defence that God affords us unless he grants consent. We are his. He has seen fit that we bear this suffering and yet we question not his love for us. In our agony we see Christ nailed to that cross at Calvary. Was God's love for his only begotten Son in anyway lacking even though he granted man authority whereby he condemned and crucified him? No, the cross speaks of the seriousness of man's state and the intensity of God's love for man . . . . 'God so loved the world.' The cross speaks of the certainty of Christ's trust in the love of God despite receiving affliction. Whose was the greatest agony at Calvary, the Father's or the Son's?

I cannot understand the 'why' of our state, but each morning as we weep and plead that this cup be taken from us, Judy and I are aware of a weeping God attending us. He does not give out his cups of sorrow easily to his servants, those he so dearly loves. What he wishes to achieve through our little boy or through us or through those who are witness to this sadness, must be of immense importance for him to demand such drastic measures, and in so many ways we receive confirmation amid our confusion, that this is of God.

The agony of heart in every area of our life is at breaking point, but in every area God is there. His grace has been sufficient and we trust him for tomorrow's manna. The sunshine has gone, we are in darkness, we cannot see our way ... not one step; but he is there.

We plead our cause with such intensity, and yet pray that we will have the trust required not to withhold Christopher should God truly desire to take him. Nothing, however, stops that continual prayer to God in what is our Gethsemane, 'Take this cup from our little boy, from his sisters, from us.' We know he can, we know God is able.

I close the piano and put away Christopher's books and long for the sound of his little melodies drifting through the house. I tidy his toys and see his ball in the garden and my heart breaks again and sorrows like sea billows roll as I hunger to have our happy days back. My heart aches at the thought of the suffering of my little lad, at the tears of his sister, now my companion, and the exhaustion of my dear wife and yet and yet … 'I know whom I have believed, and am persuaded that he is able.'

God is love, I know, I feel,
Jesus lives and loves us still.
Charles Wesley

CHAPTER 8

STRUGGLING

Sunday arrived. I had already planned to preach on the enormity of Christ's love before the events of Tuesday, using probably the most well known text in the Bible, John 3:16, 'For God so loved the world that he gave his only begotten Son, that whosoever believes in him should not perish, but have everlasting life.' What I didn't realise was the added power that the message would have because of what had happened to our family that week. It was like a theatre stage where the backdrop behind the actors changes and completely transforms what the audience is watching even though the actors haven't changed. The backdrop of this message was now totally different to what it would have been.

As I presented my text, I sensed that those in the congregation were wondering what I would say about God's love in the light of all that had happened. Also, I had never anticipated the fact that a whole group of strangers, people holidaying in the area, would join us for worship and be deeply affected by what they discovered and heard, and that they would never forget that morning.

Eventually, as news travelled, we discovered that people were praying all over the world for our little lad, people we had never heard of. We even had a letter from a group of ladies in Malawi who told us how they were continually praying for him. Cards and notes were regularly pushed through our letterbox from people living in the village; strangers would stop me in the street and ask after him or express their concern. Some of them wondered why God would allow something like that to happen to people like us? They had always assumed that Christian people had some sort of protection, like an insurance policy, some sort of immunity from the woes that others experienced. I was given countless opportunities to speak of a Saviour who entered our world and shared our woes, and who then called his servants to follow him and share the woes of others.

Sometimes some well-meaning person would say something foolish or insensitive in a feeble attempt to comfort us. On more than one occasion an anger would rise up in me that would soon turn to pity as the thought arose, 'Forgive them for they know not what they say.' Just one example: A Christian lady I knew came up to me and asked after Christopher and the family and then said,

'God is so good. He knows what he is doing,' and I agreed with her, but wondered about her reason for saying it.

'You may be losing your son, but God in his mercy is providing a replacement by giving you twins!'

I couldn't believe my ears. There was no certainty that we were going to lose our little lad. Although there was a long way to go when that dear lady said what she said, Christopher had already begun chemotherapy and was starting his radiotherapy, and the signs were that he was entering remission. In addition, the implication of what she said was of a God playing games, a God for whom Christopher was not of any particular worth; that he was expendable and replaceable. She was obviously talking about a God who was very different to the one I knew. I bit my lip, smiled and walked away.

After just over six weeks they allowed Christopher to come home for weekends, and four weeks later he came home to stay. We had booked a fortnight's holiday in Bournemouth before all of this began, but following his diagnosis and hospitalisation we had not known whether to cancel it or not. We didn't know whether he would be with us or not, in hospital or not. Fortunately, the hospital in Liverpool managed to organise the treatment he needed at a hospital near to where we were staying while we were away. Christopher's hair had fallen out and he felt embarrassed so he chose to have a small cloth cap to cover his baldness. The first week at the seaside he had a great time. Much of it was spent on the beach with him running in and out of the water, playing in the sand. I commented to Judy that he seemed to have more energy than before he was ill! Then, quite suddenly, at the weekend, he began to be sick.

The following week, day after day, confined to bed, he just kept vomiting; a reaction to his chemotherapy. Either Judy or I would sit all day by his bedside whilst the other one took Sarah and Naomi out to enjoy the sunshine. We knew that it was temporary and each day hoped it would all be over the following day. It never was. Saturday, the day of our departure, came and we had a horrendous journey home, stopping every twenty miles or so for him to be sick even though he had very little in his stomach to be sick with. A journey that should have taken us just over four hours, took well over twice that time. We all arrived home exhausted; never was there such relief to see our front door. We thanked the Lord for our safe arrival. The following day Christopher's vomiting stopped!

Judy, in the meantime, was getting very large. Among the many cards received, one stood out from the others. It was hand painted with a beautiful verse in it. With the fact that my car would soon be too small to transport our family with its anticipated additions, I purchased an old van and had it converted to a caravanette (a campervan). One day a local man, who became a good friend, was servicing it outside his home when a woman, probably in her forties, came walking along the pavement, stopped, talked with my friend and then said one or two things to me as though she knew me, before then going into his house.

'Who's that,' I asked my friend.

'Christine,' he replied.

'Christine?' I said.

'Yes, the woman who sent you that hand painted card you told me about,' he added.

'Why didn't you tell me? I could have thanked her for it.' My friend had returned to concentrating on what he was doing. His head was again under the bonnet of my van and he didn't answer. Shortly afterwards the woman left the house and as she walked by I called out to her.

'Sorry Christine, I didn't know who you were or else I would have thanked you for that beautiful card and the very apt poem inside it.'

'That's OK, glad you liked it,' she said, 'how's your little boy doing.'

'He's actually doing quite well. The treatment isn't very nice to say the least, and we are having to journey to Liverpool twice a week at present, but he is in remission and back at school, praise the Lord. Reading the card you sent, I can see that you are obviously a Christian. Where do you worship?' The minute I asked the question I knew that I had embarrassed her.

'Err ... I don't go anywhere,' she answered sheepishly.

'Have you ever been to The Salvation Army?' I then asked.

'No,' she replied, 'but I have heard of it,' she added.

'Well tomorrow is our harvest festival. You would be more than welcome to come and join with us. We are small in number, but a very friendly lot, and God does come and bless us. If you decide to come, but after a few minutes decide that it isn't for you, feel free to leave. No one will chase you or try and drag you back!' I said with a grin. She laughed, thanked me and said that she would think about it. She then walked away and said goodbye to us. My friend said nothing. His head was still under the bonnet of my vehicle.

The following day Christine came to worship. She didn't leave early, she stayed until the end and the following week her husband Joerg joined her. They had been brought up in a Christian community that had commenced in Germany in 1920. It now had communities in the USA, Germany, the UK and Australia. It was started by an idealist, a man who wanted to create a group whose communal living was based on the early church in Jerusalem, where the church members were of 'one heart and mind, and shared all things in common' (Acts 4:32). Those who belong to the community do not have any private property or a salary or a bank account; everything is shared. Any personal income or income from the community's various businesses is pooled and used for the care of all members and the community's outreach efforts.

This all sounds fine, and at the beginning, to a degree, it was. But even back then there were aspects of the community's life that were highly questionable. To challenge or question the word of the leaders was considered rebellious to both the community and to God. Such 'rebels' were treated to cruel punishment like being kept apart from the rest of the community. They were even prohibited from communicating with family members. The idea behind this was that the 'discipline' would encourage the 'rebel' to comply. I was told of a pregnant woman who was ostrasized from the rest of the community and forced to gather stones from the fields every day because of a misdemeanour committed or a rule broken. This lasted a long time and happened despite her growing size and the fact that it was the middle of winter!

Also, following the death of the founder, his descendants took control so that the leadership today is very much a dynastic thing with the members very much 'controlled.' All this caused a rift within the membership with many damaged members leaving, some disillusioned with the community and others, more seriously, disillusioned with Christianity. Yet, the community present an image of authentic Christianity to the world outside and claim that loving one

71

another is at the centre of their organisation.

The man who serviced my car was German. He like Christine, had been brought up in the community. He, his foster parents and two brothers were ejected from the community following years of harsh treatment, and when they left they forfeited everything they had, they left with nothing. My friend's younger brother managed to get a job on a farm, but was then killed when his tractor turned over and crushed him. My friend always blamed the cause of his brother's death on the situation he was placed in as a result of him being ejected from the community. Consequently, I discovered him to be bitter and angry with anything to do with religion.

Joerg and Christine had left the community with nothing following a very long period of difficulty during which the leadership refused their requests to marry with no explanation. Ejected from the only world they had ever known, they had much to learn about how best to live in their new world. They had never handled money and were strangers in an environment that was completely alien to them. They had been taught that their community was the only true biblically-based church, living as God would have Christ's followers live, and that other Christians and churches were suspect. So, although they ventured up the hill and joined us each Sunday, and enjoyed it and were much blessed by the fellowship there, they moved forward with caution, only gradually becoming more and more relaxed and alive in Christ.

My mechanic, their friend who had become my friend, was extremely kind to me, but when it came to the things of Jesus he rigidly held me at bay and became angry very easily. Despite the terrible treatment that he and his brother had received at the hands of the community, and the sense of lostness he had now that he was out of it, he could not let go of the deeply held yet ambivalent conviction that their way was the only way, and that no other church was a true church.

With the years I have discovered so many people who have

been wounded by religion or by Christians who have not been filled with the Spirit of Christ. St Paul knew the experience and I quote again his words, 'Because of you Jews, the Gentiles speak evil of God' (Romans 2:24 GNV). I don't think that is a message just for the Jews of Paul's time. How often do non-believers speak evil of God, think ill of Jesus, because of what they have observed of Christians, I wonder?

Life was tough, we were struggling on a personal level, but God was blessing us and, despite our shortcomings, there was a lovely spirit in our worship and new people were 'turning up' and feeling they had 'come home', as they put it.

With all that had happened and the reluctance of many to support the acquisition and relocating of the buildings we had been offered, I was carrying a lot of guilt. I no longer had the time or energy needed to bring the plans to fruition. With the opposition and lack of support I could see the possibility of us having a 'presence' down in that estate becoming nothing more than a pipe-dream. I prayed much about it, believing that he who could pluck a brand from the inevitability of burning (Zechariah 3:2), he who could set fire to an offering so drenched with water that it could never be ignited (1 Kings 18:33-38), could somehow do what needed to be done.

Sometimes, when I read God's word there seems to be a sense in which God goes out of his way to convince a person or persons of just how impossible a task is before he then goes and does it. He promises to make Abraham the father of many nations and then waits until neither Abraham or Sarah are at all capable of having children before he miraculously fulfils his promise. Another glimpse of this principle is seen in John 6, when Jesus asks Philip where they might get food to feed the approaching hungry crowd. Jesus knew they did not have the money needed to buy a large amount of food, and he also already knew what he was going to do about the problem (v. 6). But he wanted Philip to realise the impossibility of the task before he set about doing the impossible, feeding over 5,000 people with just five loaves and two fish.

Months were passing by in my own impossible situation. I prayed much that God might do something, give me someone to help. Eventually I received yet another telephone call from the chemical works asking how things were progressing and how long it would be before the buildings were removed? Their removal was now becoming an urgent issue, and I didn't know what to do.

CHAPTER 9

SURPRISE, SURPRISE, SURPRISE

'Sorry to wake you but I feel so dreadful. I've been back and forth to the bathroom all night being sick,' I heard Judy say as I roused from my slumber. Before my eyes could fully adjust to the light she had switched on, I looked at the clock and read 5.30 am. When I finally focused on Judy, she certainly looked pretty poorly, and with her being now thirty-five weeks pregnant, I was even more concerned than I might otherwise be.

'Have you taken anything?' I asked.

'No, I was too frightened to as I didn't know what effect it might have on the babies.' Again she went off to the bathroom feeling another bout was imminent. I wasn't sure quite what to do but knew that there would be someone at our doctor's surgery at 8 am who would be able to advise us.

'Were you sick again?' I asked as we met on the landing.

'No, I thought I was going to be but I wasn't.'

'Do you think you ate something that disagreed with you?'

'I wouldn't think so. We all ate the same food and you and the children haven't been affected,' she replied.

Time flew as breakfast followed our prayer time, and we then saw to the children as they each emerged from their slumbers. I got to the surgery just as our doctor arrived and told him of Judy's dreadful night.

'When was she last sick?' he asked.

'About an hour and a half ago,' I replied.

'I am not happy to give her anything. Are you in a position to get her to the hospital? I would prefer them to see her and prescribe something,' he said. I responded positively and he added, 'then I'll write you a note and also ring them to tell them you are coming.'

I thanked him and left.

Having got the two eldest children off to school, I popped round a neighbour's house to see if they could look after Naomi who had had her first birthday only a few weeks earlier. The neighbour was happy to have her and so we were able to leave promptly for the hospital.

Arriving on the maternity unit, we were ushered into an unoccupied four bedded area and Judy was told to lie on the bed. The sister in charge then attached a monitor to her right arm, telling us that it would save time as the doctor would want to know exactly what was going on inside her. We never thought to ask what it was that was being monitored. After some time, the sister came back to reassure us that Judy hadn't been forgotten but that the registrar had been called away on an emergency. Neither of us had thought to bring a book to read or something to do. Time seemed to drag. I was just glad that since leaving the house Judy had not been sick again.

'This is typical,' she said, 'like going to the dentist with a terrible toothache that stops the moment you walk into the dentist's waiting room. I bet the doctor will think I have been making it up,' she added.

'Why would he do that?' I asked. 'Besides which, I bet it's left you sore, hasn't it?'

'It has left me very sore. I feel so tired too. I wonder what the doctor is going to give me?'

As we chatted and waited we heard the monitor that Judy was

76

connected to make a loud 'clunk' sound. When we looked we noticed that the pen that had previously been drawing gentle curves had gone right to the end of the paper where it seemed to have got stuck.

'I wonder what has happened?' Judy exclaimed.

'You've probably broken it,' I said, and we both laughed.

Less than a minute later the registrar appeared with a couple of nursing staff, said hello to us, apologised to us for having been kept waiting for a couple of hours then, looking first at the monitor and then at Judy asked, 'Are you feeling all right Mrs Webber?'

'Why?' she asked, somewhat alarmed.

'I think you have started. Pull the curtains nurse. Please wait outside, Mr Webber.'

Suddenly panic set in, 'I'd better call Olwen to let her know that we might not be back in time for the children leaving school. I'll ask her if she can get someone to meet them if we fail to return,' I said to Judy, now out of sight behind the curtains that had been drawn. 'I'll make sure she can keep Naomi with her until we get back,' I added. Obeying the doctor, I then scurried out of the area calling out, 'I won't be long love,' as I left.

Unfortunately, I didn't have Olwen's telephone number with me, but in the corridor outside the ward there was a public telephone together with a telephone directory. This was to be my first experience of trying to find a particular 'Jones' in a North Wales telephone directory! There were pages and pages of Jones. Oh that I had asked for their telephone number before I left. Olwen's husband's name was Idris, so the task of finding their number should have been an easy one, but I scoured every 'Jones' whose first name starting with the letter 'I' all to no avail. None of the ones I found lived at Olwen's address.

'Are they ex-directory?' I wondered, 'but why would they not want to be in the telephone directory? What am I to do? I'm going to have to go through every single 'Jones,' I thought. It took ages before I discovered a 'Jones' with their address … 'Hallelujah!' It turned out that Idris was not his first name. The directory had the letter 'I' as the initial of his *second* name. 'Typical,' I thought. I should have guessed. I already knew several people in the village who were known by their second name rather than their first one. My treasurer Russell was one of them. His first name was David. Idris was obviously another one!

Having eventually spoken to Olwen to ensure that our three children would be cared for, I returned to the ward and the four bedded unit to find it empty. 'Where was Judy?' I wondered. I went in search of the ward sister only to discover that a new one had come on duty in my absence, and that she did not know what I was talking about when I asked the whereabouts of my wife. However, she did offer to ring the labour ward to find out for me.

'Yes ... Mrs Webber,' she said to the person at the other end of the phone, 'she's expecting twins.' After a few minutes wait she responded to whatever was being said at the other end, 'it's imminent you say? ... I'll send Mr Webber right away, thank you.' Putting the phone back on the receiver she turned to me and said, 'Apparently your twins are on their way and seem to be in a hurry! Do you know where the labour ward is?'

'Yes,' I replied, 'I was there just over a year ago for the birth of our last baby.'

'Well you had better hurry then Mr Webber or you'll miss it all.'

Having entered the anteroom of the labour ward, I discovered a nurse waiting to help me put on a white gown and plastic overshoes before ushering me into what seemed to be a rather crowded room. Even though Christopher had been transferred to the specialist children's hospital in Liverpool some months earlier, doctors and other staff at the ante natal clinic always asked Judy how he was doing. The hospital showed care and concern for the whole of the family, not just the individual they were dealing with. Sudden news of these impending births must have travelled rapidly around the hospital, for even the consultant paediatrician who had initially investigated and diagnosed Christopher's illness was there, as well as other doctors and nursing staff. I never did discover who they all were. Certainly, we had never had such a crowd at any of Judy's previous three deliveries. Maybe some of the 'extras' present were there because it was twins, who knows?

I went over to Judy and had hardly spoken to her before she was asked to give one last push.

'Yes, it's a girl!' someone cried out, and before I knew what had happened they placed this slimy little blue thing, wrapped in a white sheet, into my arms.

'A third daughter,' I thought,' wow!' as I looked in wonder at the lovely little thing with its tiny fingers and toes, flat nose and wrinkled forehead. Meanwhile poor Judy still had work to do. I stood close so that she could see the first product of her labours whilst she concentrated on bringing the other one into the world.

'Stop, stop, wait a minute Mrs Webber, we just want to check everything is all right. I know it's hard, but please don't push … not for a moment.' A minute went by. Standing close to Judy I was unable to see what they were doing. She gave me something resembling a smile as she looked at baby number one, before the midwife at the bottom of her delivery bed told her that all was OK and that she could now push again. I've never got over the way that Judy has always been so quiet whenever she has been in labour. Despite all the strain of pushing and all the pain, she rarely ever made even a whimper.

With one boy and three girls now, I just wondered what this last arrival would be. Then suddenly the cry went up, 'It's another girl,' and Judy half laughed and half cried at the relief.

'Are they all right?' she asked.

'Perfectly OK,' the doctor replied, placing a second slimy little blue thing, wrapped in a white sheet, into my other arm. 'So what have you got to say, Mr Webber?' he asked me.

I looked at one bundle and then the other, 'They're amazing,'

I replied, 'and to think we only came in for a bottle of medicine to stop Judy being sick.' This was met by convulsions of laughter from everyone in the room, … well everyone that is except poor Judy. She wasn't in a very good condition and needed some stitches. One of the nurses took first one baby and then another from me to be weighed and measured before returning them to Judy to hold, whilst they saw to the stitching.

'I think you're brilliant,' I said. Judy responded with a smile which she then radiated to her two new daughters. She was obviously in a lot of discomfort, but she was also so very proud.

'We are going to have to put them both into incubators, nothing to be alarmed at. They are premature and we have detected a little breathing problem in them both, but we are sure they will be OK,' the doctor said. Both twins had breathing and feeding problems at first and they and mummy remained in the hospital for a week, with me bringing the other three children to see their two new sisters.

Christopher was much better in himself and his hair was gradually re-growing. He had a daily dose of tablets and continued to visit the hospital in Liverpool every week, but he was back at school and doing all the things young ten year old boys do. He was in remission but it would be quite some time before we knew that he was out of the woods.

As the corps centenary year came to a conclusion we had a celebratory weekend like we had done when it began. On the Sunday that the special year commenced our two month old daughter, Naomi, had been dedicated to God[10] and now, a year later, at its conclusion, our one month old twins were dedicated to God. On both oc-

---

10   Whereas most churches have either the baptism or christening of an infant, The Salvation Army has a dedication ceremony, where the parents dedicate their little one to God, as Hannah did Samuel, (1 Samuel 1: 25-28). The ceremony includes thanksgiving to God for the gift God has given them, and a promise to keep from the child all that would harm the child in body, mind or spirit, to teach the truths of the gospel, encouraging the child to seek Christ as Saviour, and to be an example of a Christian to the child.

casions we sent personal invitations to the dedications to the many non-believers we had got to know ... and they came. On both occasions the hall was packed and the people came under the message of the gospel.

Not long after the twins were born, a man of the road named Maldwyn started to regularly attend our worship with his little dog. Maldwyn was a short man with jet black hair, aged about fifty years. He was also a very quiet man, amenable, but so quiet and unobtrusive that you would hardly notice he was there. His dog was very similar and during worship would lay quite motionless under his chair. I discovered that Maldwyn slept in a farmer's barn in a village some four miles from ours and that he walked all the way to our hall and back again each Sunday. At various times people offered to take him back in their cars at the conclusion of the meetings but he always declined their offers. I also discovered that the farmer was very kind to him, giving him hot meals and other food from time to time.

Have you ever asked someone a question only to discover that the reply has put an onus on you? As we entered what was to be our last December, I went and sat with him after worship one Sunday morning before he got up to leave. I asked him one or two questions in an effort to know him and understand him better. He seemed reluctant to say much and I didn't catch all that he did say but was too embarrassed to keep saying, 'Pardon? Pardon?' However, when I asked him what he was going to do for Christmas, the reply came back quite clearly,

'Nothing.'

'Are you spending it on your own then?' I enquired.

'Yes,' he answered.

'Don't you have any friend who you could spend it with?' I then asked.

'No,' he replied, 'don't have any friends.'

His reply saddened me, but also challenged me. 'But what could we do about it?' I thought as the limited conversation came to an end and we went our separate ways. 'Our council house isn't very big and there is already insufficient room around our dining table or in the lounge for all seven of us, what with all the babies' paraphernalia, never mind any Christmas toys the children may want to play with!'

One moment I was happy, unaware that Maldwyn would be alone. Then, one simple question later, everything changed. I had assumed he had some friend, some buddy, or even that the farmer would take him in for a few hours, but now I knew differently and I could not 'unknow' what I now knew. I prayed and tried to reason myself off the hook as I walked home, but I got no peace. Over the lunch table, whilst I held both milk bottles to the gurgling twins and Judy helped Naomi with her dinner, (when she wasn't picking up food debris from the carpet under Naomi's high chair), I shared with Judy what Maldwyn had said. Her response was immediate. There was no question of him being on his own. Maldwyn was to come to our house for the day.

'It will be a squash, he'll have to accept us as we are, but if he wants to come then we would be pleased to have him,' she said. So it was that he came to Christmas morning worship and then walked down the long footpath to our home with his dog. It was a bitterly cold day, but fairly warm once we were indoors. There wasn't much room around the table and we did not have enough chairs, but we could tell that he was thoroughly enjoying himself. He pulled crackers with us and put on his paper hat, before tucking into his roast turkey with all its trimmings and then his Christmas pudding. With our noisy brood we were unable to pay him much attention, but he seemed quite happy watching all that was going on at our entertaining table.

After lunch, when all the crockery and cutlery was washed and wiped up and put away, we joined Maldwyn in the lounge where he was sat up in the corner, close to the fire. The twins were asleep in their cots upstairs and the other three children were playing with their new toys and asking mum and then dad to help them with some newfangled plaything or to join them in their play. The radio produced a variety of Christmas music in the background. Maldwyn just sat there, silent, mesmerised by it all. I can't really explain it, but although he did nothing and hardly said anything, Maldwyn seemed to bring something quite lovely into our home. Somehow, I know not how, he affected the two of us, though we were only to discover it when we conversed after he had gone.

We were still quite full from our Christmas lunch so we did not want too much to eat when tea-time came following the twins' afternoon nap. But no sooner had we finished our cups of tea than Maldwyn said, 'I'll be off now.'

'Let me take you home,' I insisted.

'No, I'll walk,' he replied.

'Are you sure? It's very dark and cold, and the road isn't well lit. Please let me take you back,' I said a bit more forcefully.

'No, I want to walk. I prefer to walk.' As we helped him on with his heavy coat he thanked us both and said how much he had enjoyed it, and we opened the door and watched him and his little dog go up the garden path and out of sight.

It was as we lay in bed that night talking over the day that we discovered that both of us had felt the same about Maldwyn's day with us, and both of us felt emotional as we agreed that though he just sat there, did nothing, said hardly a word, he had done so much more for us than we had done for him. Then we remembered the scripture that says, 'Do not forget to entertain strangers, for by doing so some people have entertained angels without knowing it' (Hebrews 13:2). What a wonderful God of surprises we have.

'I have to say that this has been one of the loveliest Christmas Days I have ever known, thank you Jesus, good night love, sleep tight.'

'Yes, it certainly has. I love you. Night, night.'

83

CHAPTER 10

ONE INTERWOVEN STORY

'Would you like a picture of your General?' asked a middle-aged man with his pint of lager in his hand.

'My General?' I asked the stranger, for whom I was aware that the pint in his hand was not the first that evening.

'Yes,' he replied, 'White beard and everything.'

I wasn't too sure that the man was serious. I wondered whether he was teasing me, or whether indeed he did have a picture but that it was a case of mistaken identity. I assumed he was talking about The Salvation Army's founder, General William Booth, but wondered, (if there was a picture), whether it was some other bearded character, Charles Darwin, Abraham Lincoln or even Santa Claus! Not wanting to dismiss and upset the man I asked, 'Where did you get it?'

'I found it in the loft of Garth chapel,' he responded.

'Garth chapel loft?' I questioned.

'Yes, my wife and I bought the chapel and are renovating it and turning it into a house for us to live in. We found the picture when we were rooting about in the loft. Would you like to see it? I could bring it here and show you?' he added.

'OK,' I said, somewhat intrigued and bemused, 'Thank you.'

Leaving, I went from public house to public house down one side of the Dee Valley, then around the town of Llangollen before travelling back along the other side, distributing the War Cry at each hostelry as I went. With everything that transpired that evening and the many conversations along the way, further thought of that encounter was soon erased from my mind. Even when I was greeted by the same man a week later, as I re-entered the Australian Arms, it took a moment or two to realise what he was talking about when he told me he had the picture in the boot of his car and would show it to me when I finished my visit.

We walked across the road to where he had parked his car and he opened the boot, untied the string around the plastic he had wrapped it in, to reveal a large unframed picture portrait of General William Booth. It was in very good condition.

'Would you like it?'

'Yes, I would,' I answered. 'How on earth did it ever get into the loft of Garth chapel?' I asked him.

'I've no idea,' was his reply.

'I hope that you don't think it cheeky, but could you have another look in your chapel loft and see if there is one the same size, of a lady? This portrait is one of a matching pair of William and his wife Catherine. She is often referred to as the Mother of The Salvation Army.' Thanking him, we parted. We met up several times over the coming weeks, and despite searching the chapel thoroughly he was never able to find the other matching portrait.

I showed the picture to Russell and he offered to get it framed so that it could be hung at the back of our worship hall. 'I know a picture-framer who would do a good job, he said, 'and his prices are reasonable. He's a nice guy and wouldn't rip us off.' Consequently, the picture was beautifully framed and hung at the back of our hall.

It was some months later that I received a telephone call from a very anxious man telling me that his wife had gone missing, probably had run away and left him, but that he had received a telephone message from the police that she was at The Salvation Army somewhere. He was concerned about the state she was in when she vanished and whether she was all right. He asked me if I knew anything about it. I replied that I didn't, but assured him that I would try and find out where she was and how she was and would get back to him.

Initially, I presumed that she was in one of our women's hostels, the nearest being either in Liverpool or Birmingham, but phone calls to both proved disappointing. I then commenced ringing various corps in the region, starting with the closest. After four or five calls I found that she had been befriended by The Salvation Army officer in Chester. Although I was then able to ring her husband John very late at night to say that I knew where she was and that she was safe, at that stage I dared not tell him where she was.

It was at 9 o'clock in the evening that Lieutenant Elwyn Harries received a telephone call from a woman, somewhat distraught, who had tried to drown herself in the River Dee. However, having waded into the deep, fast moving waters, she had lacked the courage to go through with what she intended. On leaving the river soaking wet she had got on the first bus that came along. The bus just happened to be going to Chester. When she got there, whilst in a telephone kiosk looking for the number for the Samaritans in the telephone directory, she saw the name 'Salvation Army' which appeared just before 'Samaritans,' so she telephoned their number instead.

Upon receiving Jane's call, Elwyn immediately left home and met up with her. For a long time he just sat and listened in silence as she shared her story and her sense of hopelessness, after which he was able to offer encouragement and support, managing to get her into the Sisters of Chester Cathedral Retreat House overnight. It was a lovely place of peace that was run by nuns. However, that peace was much disturbed in the early hours by the arrival of police officers who woke Jane, wanting to confirm that it was indeed her who was staying there.

Jane had had an affair with a close friend of her husband, a married man, who she had come to love deeply. The affair had come to an end but they remained in regular telephone contact. John knew nothing of the affair until she broke it to him that fateful day, the day she went missing. What caused her to tell her husband about it was the unexpected, devastating news they received that day that her husband John had been diagnosed with lymphoma.

Jane was already in an emotional maelstrom and under the care of a psychiatrist. The added news of John's illness just tipped the scales, resulting in such a sense of guilt that all she wanted to do, following her confession, was end her life. In fact she had an appointment with her psychiatrist at Wrexham hospital the day following her bus journey to Chester, and when Elwyn discovered this, he kindly offered to take her there.

'Would you like me to change out of my uniform?' he asked her.

'Why? Are you ashamed of it?' Jane replied.

'No, of course not. I just didn't want to be an embarrassment to you.'

Having had a restful night and a chance to gather her thoughts together, Jane agreed that her husband John meet up with her at the hospital and accompany her to the psychiatrist. At the end of the meeting Elwyn said good-bye to them both and returned to Chester as John and Jane returned to their home together.

About a month later, in December, our band was playing Christmas carols in Oswestry. It was freezing cold as several of us stood along the high street with our collecting tins, rubbing our hands and occasionally jumping up and down to keep warm. It's illegal to shake our collection boxes, but jumping up and down to keep warm makes the coins rattle anyway! A lady came up to me and put a five pound note in my box and then expressed how grateful she was to The Salvation Army for what it had done for her. Asking her a few questions about herself I discovered that it was Jane, the very lady I had tried to find as a result of that phone call from her husband weeks earlier. After a brief conversation and an offer to be of any further help to her in the future, she went on her way.

In the afternoon, following a break to rest our legs and eat our packed lunches, there were as many collectors as there were shoppers on the High Street, so I took myself to the back entrance of the store I had been standing outside. I couldn't hear the band playing its carols when I got there, but felt that I could give directions to where they were to anyone who asked, and that even without the band I might do well with no other collectors in sight. I had not been there very long when a man wandered up to me and asked,

'Are you pleased with your picture?'

'Pleased with my picture?' I answered, taken aback by the strangeness of the question and uncertain as to what he was talking about.

'Yes, your picture. I framed a picture of your founder, William Booth. I think it hangs at the back of your hall. I'm a friend of Russell's and I saw him playing in the band a few moments ago and he said you were here somewhere.'

'Oh, you're the guy,' I replied, 'Thank you so much. You did a great job. We're very grateful. It looks good.' After a little more conversation, he put some money in my box, we shook hands and he departed.

Sometime later, having looked at my watch and realised that our carolling for the day would soon be finished, I walked through the store and out the other end. No sooner had I emerged than I saw Jane and the man I had been speaking to, the man who framed our picture, walking arm in arm towards where I was standing.

'Do you two know each other?' I asked them both.

'We should, we've been married seventeen years,' they

laughed. We then talked together and towards the end of the conversation they shared with me how they intended to travel to Chester and attend the Christmas carol service at the corps there. They were so grateful to Elwyn for all he had done. 'If, however, the weather is too bad we will come to your corps instead as it's only a few miles from the village where we live. We have both decided that we want to go to a carol service this year,' said Jane.

The weather was bad that Sunday night and both John and Jane came to our carol service rather than travel the extra twenty miles to Chester. They did go to Chester corps a couple of times after Christmas, but they decided to make our corps their spiritual home. We were a few weeks into the new year when I received a late telephone call from John, telling me that the wife of Jane's former lover had only just found out about their affair and that in her fury she had been to John and Jane's shop and attacked Jane. Jane was furious that despite their agreement to tell their respective partners what they had been doing, the woman's husband had failed to do so. Consequently Jane, who had been simmering with anger all day, left home that evening intent on smashing all the windows in the man's home. John wondered whether I could go out there and stop her! The man had been John's closest friend and so he had his address. It was quite late at night but I agreed to go, even though I had no idea of what I would do when I got there.

It was gone 10.30 pm when I arrived, and from where I parked the car I could see that all the windows at the front of the house were still intact. I parked away from the lamplight under a tree and against a hedge, in the hope that I would not be noticed from the house ... or any other house for that matter. The last thing I wanted was for anyone to ring the police because they had seen a suspicious character sitting in a car in the dark watching someone's house! I had a job keeping awake. I was tired and got very cold, but I dare not switch the engine on to warm the car for fear of the noise it would make. I sat there three hours awaiting what I thought would be an explosive drama, but it never happened. There were moments when I caught a glimpse of someone in the dark, but each time it was someone innocently walking their dog late at night or making their way home in the early hours. Eventually I decided to call it a day, (or rather a night). Pretty certain Jane was not going to turn up I made my way home to the welcome of my warm bed. When I next saw Jane she was calm. Apparently she did go out to the house, arriving before I got there, but having given more thought to what she was preparing to do, she decided better of it and went home. If only I had known.

On Good Friday morning of that year, we had a breakfast at the hall with everyone in the corps invited. The tables were arranged in a U-shape with a large rough wooden cross erected at the centre between the two end tables. Like the Last Supper the meal was eaten in the shadow of the cross, after which all attention was focused on what the death of Jesus on the cross meant to each of us. People were encouraged to bring and share anything they liked as long as it was related to Good Friday and Christ dying on the cross. It could be a poem or hymn or a recording of music. It could be scripture or just thoughts that occurred as a person meditated on God's great and amazing act of saving grace. A powerful sense of the Spirit of God descended upon the gathering as we finished the meal and, with the bowls, plates, cups and cutlery, uneaten toast and packets of cereal still on the tables, one by one people made their contributions.

Maldwyn, with his dog asleep under his chair, sat there quietly, listening to each person's contribution. He had never spoken in public. In fact he rarely said anything at all. It came as a surprise to us all when he suddenly spoke out and, in almost a whisper, expressed what the cross of Jesus meant to him. What this tramp, this man of the road, this hobo said so quietly yet so sincerely, was powerful … far more powerful than anyone realised at the time. For although God had been speaking very clearly to Jane, and she had been gradually responding, John had remained unmoved, defiant, anti-religious, full of well-thought-through answers to anything presented to him.

But as Maldwyn, in such a quiet and simple manner, expressed what the death of Jesus meant to him and what Jesus had done for him, something softened the hardness and melted the coldness in John's heart. On leaving that meeting that Good Friday morning and driving home along the country lanes, John opened up his heart and said to his wife, 'If God can do a work like that in his life then he can surely do the same in mine.'

Shortly after that, one Sunday morning as worship drew to a close, John and Jane came together and knelt before the Lord seeking forgiveness, accepting Jesus as their Lord and Saviour, and committing themselves to loving and serving him the rest of their days. There were many issues and difficulties to be dealt with, as there was still a lot of repair work to be done to their marriage; their business was failing and that was to result in them losing their home. Together they would face seven years of trials and tribulations as John battled with his lymphoma, a cancer that would turn out to be terminal. But they had found Jesus. As they were both to testify on many an occasion – that changed everything.

CHAPTER 11

INTO THE FIRE

Having gone over and over all that had happened during the previous three years, I was no nearer a solution as to why Miss Barrett told me, 'You are the worst officer this corps has ever had,' than when she said it. I, with my wife, had worked hard amid some trying circumstances. We felt we had not just done a job, but that we had given ourselves to the village and corps. We were in no doubt that God had blessed our offering. New people had come to Christ and become a real part of our worshipping community. The spirit in the corps was continually improving and we had seen God do some truly remarkable things.

Yes, there were things left undone, things that I regretted. We left with the two buildings that we were offered eighteen months earlier still standing in the chemical works. The works manager had become understandingly impatient at the fact that despite our plans, we had done nothing about moving them. The last twelve months had been such a struggle that I could not apply either the time or the thinking required to take the project forward as I might have done had our circumstances been different. There were also personnel changes that needed to be made that I hadn't made. Again, our family difficulties had taken so much of my time as well as my emotional and physical energy ... or were my reasons merely excuses for my ineptitude?

We had received our marching orders[11] soon after Easter with, as it was in those days, six weeks notice to pack and prepare for the move. Following my visit to Miss Barrett, all we had was a couple more weeks to go before we left on the short thirty-eight mile journey to our new home and life. We were sad to go. There were some truly lovely, supportive people in the corps and village, and we had shared some wonderful times together, times of joy and times of sadness. In addition, the Lord had taught us so much about himself that would hold us in such good stead in the future.

We arrived at our new home, so different to the council house we had left an hour or so earlier. It was a four bedroom villa-style semi-detached house, built at the beginning of the twentieth century, with large rooms and high ceilings. But the condition of the house and its furnishing left much to be desired. There were large cracks in the walls of a number of the rooms. In fact we could see the garden through one such crack that ran from the corner of the window to the floor in the dining room! A surveyor had inspected the property prior to our arrival and had then recommended that a structural engineer with more expertise be called. On thoroughly inspecting the house the structural engineer announced the news that our home was suffering from severe subsidence, and that the entire side wall of the house would need to be underpinned. And that was not all. Whilst inspecting the loft, the engineer discovered that the joists holding the main bedroom ceiling were at the very edges of the bricks, and that any slight movement of the wall might send the

---

[11] Salvation Army Officers do not apply for a position like one would in normal employment, but agrees to go wherever the army decides to send them, whenever it decides it is time for them to go. Although there is discussion beforehand about each personal situation and schooling and health and family concerns are prayerfully considered, the final decision is confirmed when Marching Orders are received.

whole lot crashing down on us. (Since our arrival we had often laid in bed looking up at the ceiling and wondered what was the cause of it being so bowed. Now we knew).

'If it were me,' the man said, 'I would not want to spend one night under that.'

That was all the warning we needed. We spent most of the rest of the day moving our bed and furniture into the next biggest room which we would then share with two of the children for the next nine months. With both their beds and ours, there was little room for both sets of furniture so we had to put one set on top of the other. The two girls that we shared the room with thought it great fun at bed time, having to clamber over our bed to get to theirs, often using it as a trampoline on the way ... of course!

As if all this wasn't enough to contend with, when we first entered the dining room and then looked round the kitchen, we were surprised to find that the windows in both appeared to be of frosted glass or else suffering from an acute degree of condensation. We were unable to see out of them. Wiping the inside and the outside of the panes, we discovered that whatever the cause, it was between the panes of the double glazing. Using a chisel, I managed to very care-fully remove the outer panes of the two windows, only to discover that what I thought was condensation between the panes was the re-sult of a chemical etching that had occurred when the seal, of what should have been a sealed unit, had blown. There was nothing I could do about it. The sealed units would need to be replaced and, (you've got it), the corps had no money.

There were other problems regarding the house. It seemed to us that the mixture of furniture that we had inherited were other people's throw-outs. There was nothing of quality in the house. Jok-ingly, I suggested to Judy that the reason it was in our house was be-cause our house was a lot closer to town than the council's rubbish tip! She wasn't amused.

We arrived at the end of May, and so our priority was getting the two oldest children into school. Once that was done, we set about sorting things out and unpacking the boxes whilst the twins crawled about on the carpet and Naomi played with some of her toys. Imagine our shock and horror when the next mealtime arrived and we picked up the twins only to discover that the fronts of the all-in-one baby-grows, clean on that day, were filthy. We had not realised the carpets were filthy. Judy just broke down and wept. Two questions entered my mind: how could anyone have left the house in that condition for their successors and secondly, knowing our situation, how could the powers-that-be have sent us there in the first place? That second question would arise again and again in the weeks that followed.

We received a warm welcome from the corps, but soon discovered that it was beset with problems. The numbers attending had dropped off considerably over the previous few years and a number of leaders had resigned. There was no bandmaster, no Sunday school leader, no leader for the Over 60s club, and the songster leader had handed in his resignation just ahead of our arrival. There were debts and financial problems. The building, built in the 60s, was in need of a lot of repair works, including sorting out the problems of the leaks in the flat roof of the secondary hall.

I was surprised to see so few people at worship that first Sunday, other than those in the songsters and band. The hall had the capacity to seat two hundred. I felt as though I was preaching to the chairs. Most people were lovely and very sympathetic to our situation, but I soon began to hear some critical voices. One spoke of our limitations, what with my wife pre-occupied with our infants and me taking time out every week to take my son to hospital.

'What this corps needed to get it out of the doldrums was two people. It needed a husband and wife who were free to give themselves one hundred per cent, and we get sent you two! I know it wasn't your fault, but it makes me mad,' said Ernie exasperatedly.

Another complained at the fact that each Sunday evening I

preached a salvation or gospel message.

'You are preaching to the saved!' he exclaimed, 'why preach salvation every Sunday night?'

'Because, even if I can't get out there to any unsaved people,' I replied, (and I certainly couldn't consider any evangelistic outreach), 'I expect God to send people to me.' This was greeted with a look of incredulity.

Criticisms were made about the meetings, the length of my sermons, and the prayer times we had at the end of the evening meetings. Some thought that we should only have such prayer times at the end of worship if someone responded to my appeals to come to the Saviour. It all weighed heavily on me. By the end of a Sunday, having conducted and preached in two meetings, taken part in a meeting we had in the open-air, and led a very lively Sunday school, I would get home utterly exhausted.

Back at home, dear Judy had made it her job to get up in the night whenever any of the children awoke, which they frequently did, to let me sleep. She felt that I could then face the world refreshed whilst she, confined to home, would cope with being over-tired as she would not be having to meet people. Consequently, exhausted, she often went to bed soon after the children. Even though it was only 8.30 pm when I got home on a Sunday night, most times she and the children would be fast asleep. The house would be silent.

Arriving home worn out, I would take off my jacket, slacken my tie, make myself a cup of tea, and find my way to the lounge where I would slump into the old and rather smelly sofa and weep. Despite encouraging words, all that ran in my head when I got home were the discouraging and disparaging remarks. There were those who I dreaded approaching me at the end of a meeting. They may have been in the minority, but somehow what they had to say stuck. As I watched them approach me as I stood at the door shaking hands with the departing congregation, I knew that whatever they might have to say as we clasped each other's hands, it wouldn't be positive.

As I sat on the sofa in our lounge, pondering all that desperately needed to be done in the corps, I realised that I did not have the hours in the week or the wherewithal needed to do it. In fact, despite having thought myself to have something between my ears and a little bit of experience, I really did not know where to start.

All I could do was cry out to God to either get me, (or rather us), out of the situation or change it. The only positive thing that I could see about us being there was that we were still within fifty miles of the specialist hospital in Liverpool where Christopher was being treated. The last thing that Christopher needed was another move! And as for God changing the situation, I could not, even in my wildest dreams, imagine how God could possibly change any of it.

As the tears rolled down my face, I just wished I could be somewhere else. What was it David the psalmist said? 'Oh that I had the wings of a dove! I would fly away and be at rest – I would flee away and stay in the desert; I would hurry to my place of shelter far from the tempest and storm' (Psalm 55:6-7). I dreamed of the home that we had left when we decided to enter this ministry. It was a beautiful house out in the Northamptonshire countryside, spacious and clean, with vast and wonderful views across the fields that spread out behind it. I thought of the lovely solid wood furniture we had sold for a pittance to be free to go anywhere for Jesus. I felt guilty for having brought my family to this. I felt guilty that I had even less time free to spend with my son. Yes, he was in remission still, but nothing was certain. What would I feel if the worst happened and I hadn't spent the time with him that I wanted or I ought?

I wanted to leave. I wanted to escape. I tried to think of a way of taking my family and leaving it all. But where could we go? When Jonah ran away to Joppa to catch a boat to Spain he had only to find one seat. I would need to find seats for seven of us!!! Our families could not take us in. Where would I find work? Would I be able to get back into my previous profession in pathology? What about Christopher's ongoing treatment, and his and Sarah's schools? These and many other thoughts swam around in my head as I looked for even a pin-prick of light in our tunnel. And there was one thought that kept coming back to me, like the ghost that it was, from the past. It dwarfed the other things that concerned me as I looked upon the impossibility of our situation, 'I need to tell you that you are the worst officer this corps has ever had!'

'If I can neither change the situation nor escape from it, the time will eventually come when we are moved from here and our successor(s) will inherit it, and I will be seen to be the one responsible for leaving it in this state. They will think that all of this is my doing or the result of my inability or neglect. It will all reflect on me.'

CHAPTER 12

CRISIS POINT

It started with a headache which gradually got worse and was totally unaffected by taking the likes of aspirin and paracetamol, etc. As I walked to the doctors, I wondered whether the man who used to beat a huge gong with a large drum stick at the beginning of Rank Organisation films had somehow got into my head, gong and all, and was in there hitting it for all he was worth. My sight too was blurred and the bright daylight seemed to hurt my eyes.

The surgery was packed with people. I had a very long wait and when I eventually got in to see the doctor he seemed agitated. Although he listened to what I had to say and gave me a cursory examination, he appeared preoccupied. I felt I had been an inconvenient imposition on his valuable and limited time. He didn't seem very interested or very concerned and just wrote me a prescription and sent me on my way. Although the surgery was less than a mile from my home, the return walk via the pharmacist's shop seemed unending. All I wanted to do when I got back home was to crawl into bed. I felt secure wrapped beneath its sheets.

However, the pain worsened. I couldn't sleep and could not

stand any noise and needed the room darkened. When I had to get out of bed I was now very shaky on my feet. In the afternoon, Judy, now quite anxious, called the doctor to tell him of my deterioration, suggesting to him that it might be meningitis, adding that the state I was in reminded her of the time when I had had it once before many years ago. That must have triggered something in the doctor's mind for he arrived at our door within minutes of Judy putting the phone down and, in what seemed to be the briefest of time, I found myself in an ambulance on my way to hospital.

I never realised before what a traumatic experience even a ride in an ambulance could be for a sick person. Every movement, every bump in the road seemed to be amplified and sent pain through my head. I felt as though my brain was suspended on gossamer threads and that with every jerk or bump it banged against the inside wall of my skull. As I lay there I wondered, how this could be happening on top of everything else? We had only been in our new location six weeks. Everything had been such a struggle. I felt that our situation could not have got worse but now this? I know that I had asked God either to get me/us out of the situation or change our situation but this was not at all what I had in mind!

Fortunately, like the first time I had it many years before, it was not the bacterial form of meningitis. The doctors reassured me that it would not leave me brain damaged, though, (as I said in my previous book), friends have since suggested otherwise. With me out of action and Judy tied up with our domestic situation headquarters had to find other people to conduct Sunday worship and take care of the corps. As each day passed I gradually began to feel better. But that improved feeling of well-being was soon dealt a body-blow with the news that Andrew[12], one of our Junior Soldiers(Junior church members), aged eleven years, had died suddenly. A tumour behind one of his eyes had been diagnosed when he was a baby and he had

---

[12]   Andrew's story is fully described in *'Meeting Jesus: Inspiring stories of modern-day evangelism'* by the same author published by Shield Books.

lost his sight in that eye as a result of the treatment. In addition, the little lad had suffered all his life with cystic fibrosis. It was only the day before his sudden death that his mother had brought him up to see me following the treatment he had had in the hyrdrotherapy bath down in the basement of the hospital. We had joked together. He had laughed and teased me at the fact that I, not he, was in bed in pyjamas, and that he, not I, was the fully clothed visitor! It was such a lovely visit.

It was another week before I was able to leave hospital and go home. It was the day of Andrew's funeral. I felt guilty that I was unable to conduct the funeral and to be there to support the family. But, in the days that followed, confined to doing nothing as I slowly gained my strength, I began to review all that we had been through over the previous weeks and months and, as I did so, I began to sense the Lord speaking to me. As I wondered about this second bout of viral meningitis and the possible rhyme or reason for it, I felt as though the Lord was saying something like this,

'Howard, you are operating as though all the problems that have assailed you and your family are your problems and, although you are always speaking to me, praying to me, questioning me, you are so busy and preoccupied with fathoming out what to do, that you are unable to stop and hear what I actually am wanting to tell you.

You are like a fly, a bluebottle, buzzing hither and thither. Even when you stop physically, your mind never settles. You left me with no choice. You keep crying out to me and whilst I hear what you say, I can't get you to hear me. There was only way I could get you to stop and hear my response to your prayers. This meningitis was my fly-swat. I knew it would be painful, I knew you wouldn't enjoy it, but I either had to do this to you or leave you buzzing round and round in circles, forever chewed up inside.'

And so, forced to sit at the Master's feet as it were, I began a journey of self-discovery and an accompanying, far deeper, understanding of God and his ways. I never heard voices or had any supernatural experiences, but it was as though God directed my thinking and answered the questions I asked with new thoughts and insights which I have recorded here as a dialogue with him. Like Martha, I loved the Lord and wanted to serve him, I wanted to please him, but there was much that I was missing. God was saying to me what he said to her centuries before, 'Howard, Howard you are worried and upset about so many things, but only one thing is needed' (Luke 10:41-42).

'Howard, why are you so perplexed and anxious?'

'Lord, you heard what Miss Barrett said to me, or rather, what she said about me?

'Howard, why have you wasted all that energy and brain space in looking for reasons as to why you couldn't possibly have been the worst officer that corps ever had? What if you are?'

'What do you mean?'

'What if you are the worst officer they ever had, or even the worst officer in The Salvation Army?'

'I don't understand what you are driving at?'

'Well, as well as endeavouring to speak through you to your listeners when you preach, I also listen to everything you say. I have heard you say on many occasions that if someone has little to give to me, whether it be time or talents or gifts or money, but surrenders it all to me, I am able to use such offerings far more wonderfully, powerfully and fruitfully than someone with riches, be it money or talents, or gifts, be they natural or spiritual, who only gives me a portion of what they possess ... did I not hear you right?'

'Err, yes Lord.'

'And do you truly believe that?'

'Err yes Lord.'

'So where is your problem with that one, Howard? Your inadequacy, your fallibility, your shortfall does not limit me. Your concern shouldn't be whether you are the best or the worst, that is all about you comparing yourself with other people. What sort of a measure is that? No, the thing that should concern you and the thing that limits what I am able to do through you is whether or not you are totally surrendered to me and do what I desire of you.'

'But it was a hurtful thing to say, and so unfair. It wounded me deeply.'

'Hurtful? Unfair? Wounded deeply? OK, I agree that it wasn't pleasant, but it was hardly nails, was it? Now to my second point. Why do you do what you do?'

'What do you mean, Lord?'

'You sold up your home, gave up your career and a decent salary to do what you are doing. Why? What is the ultimate purpose of your life? Again, what have you taught other people as being the ultimate purpose of any life?

'To bring you glory?' I asked.

'Really? Is that what all of this is about?'

'Yes.'

'How much of the glory do you want me to have?'

'All of it, one hundred per cent'

'All of it? Not even a small amount for you? A little credit here? A little acknowledgement there? Not even a little appreciation? A footnote perhaps?

'Umm ... No, all of it.'

'Then listen to what I am going to say, Howard. For the sake of argument, suppose that you are the worst officer in The Salvation Army; do you accept that if you are completely surrendered to me, your capability or incapability would have little bearing on how I could use you? ... that it isn't about what you have to offer but what you are prepared to surrender?'

'Absolutely.'

'Then consider this. If I did any great and wonderful things through you, the worst officer in The Salvation Army, who would be given the credit? Surely people would say, well it can't be Howard, it must be God! What do you think?'

105

'I see where you're coming from.'

'On the other hand, should anyone have said, (and don't worry, no-one will), that you were the best officer they have ever had, anything that I might have achieved through you would surely be partially attributed to you. You would surely have received some of the glory that you claimed you wanted for me?

'Does it really matter what anyone else makes of you and your ministry, so long as you live to please me? I promised that I would look after you. You are my child. Have I not done that in the past? Did I not vindicate you when, in the past, there were those who said all manner of evil things about you that were untrue? Remember those rumours in the village following your visit to Auntie Vin? You didn't defend yourself against those lies, did you? You left it with me … OK, the truth is that you didn't respond because you did not know how to respond. You didn't know how "to put the record straight" as you call it, as you would have liked to have done. But did you not learn anything about me from the experience?

And that is not all. There are a lot of my servants who are hurting out there, servants just like you, servants with limitations who have been treated deplorably and made to feel worthless by some quite vindictive people. Those servants are in desperate need of encouragement. You would be my ideal tool for coming alongside them in their pit of despond and asking them, "have you ever been told that you are the worst Christian/officer/minister/elder ever?" Most times the answer will be, "No," to which you can answer, "Well I have, and it may well be true! But it hasn't stopped God doing wonderful things in and through me. If he can do that through the worst, he can do even more in and through you.'

'Wow, but I don't like people thinking I am rubbish or looking down on me.'

'But Howard, you are in my hands, you are safe. I will vindicate you. I will look after you, trust me. Follow my pattern, follow my example. Look at Jesus. He came down and made himself of no reputation, he became nothing, (Philippians 2:7). Man is always trying to be *something*, always trying to elevate himself, to be recognised, appreciated, valued. He is always pushing upward, the very opposite of Jesus. Jesus trusted me and came down and in response *I* lifted him. He went to the lowest and I lifted him to the highest. Oh that I could find other such servants, willing to be *nothing*. My, there would be no end to what I could achieve through such as they!'

'I'm beginning to see more clearly now what real trust and faith is about.'

'Good, but you know what the real obstacle to that faith and trust is, Howard?'

'What is that?'

'You!!!'

'Me?'

'Yes, you … Howard Webber!'

'What do you mean?'

'What I say. You only have one problem in life and it isn't the house or the corps or your health or your lack of resources, gifts and talents … it's you. You are your only real problem.'

'Pardon?'

'You have yet to even begin to discover what it is to die with Christ, to be crucified with Christ. Do you remember when you were a teenager? Do you remember how upset you were with the man you worked for in your spare time? Even back then I was trying to get you to see it. You caught a glimpse, but you did not dig down and examine the issues in greater depth. You discovered a fault but then resorted to self-improvement like so many Christians do. It was as if a cloud cast a shadow over the vision I wanted you to have, and things didn't progress. Think about it.

CHAPTER 13

THE NEWSAGENT

When I was a teenager in need of pocket money, I got myself a job delivering newspapers before I went to school. The newsagent was a single man, an ex-paratrooper who had spent twenty-one years in the military. He was rather a coarse man and my mother was not too keen on him and quite unhappy at me spending any time in his company. Whilst he never used bad language in front of the customers who came into his shop to purchase their newspapers, sweets and cigarettes, (in fact he was most polite and amiable), things were sometimes different out in the back room early in the morning as we sorted out the papers. When, unexpectedly, several boys failed to turn up to do their paper round, the pressure he then faced as to how he was to get all the newspapers delivered to his customers would sometimes cause him to snap. The air would be blue with his cursing and ranting. He seemed oblivious to the fact that anyone wandering into the shop would be subjected to hearing the torrent of anger pouring out from that back room.

However, whilst he gave the impression of being a very hard and somewhat coarse business man, I detected a much softer side under the image he presented. I discovered him to be a very generous individual and came across instances of him secretly dispensing kindnesses to needy people, making them vow not to tell a soul. He was cautious as he did not want to be the target of one of those unscrupulous hoaxers who, with a convincing sob-story, might try and part him from his money. Nor did he want to destroy the image he conveyed of being hard and even uncaring, probably a throw back from his military past. How complex we human beings are.

Leaving school I went to work in London for a year. Returning home, I took up a post in pathology at the local hospital. Early one morning I popped into the shop and found Charlie quite stressed because several boys had failed to show up, so I offered my services. I could give him an hour if it would help him. A smile beamed across his face as he expressed his gratitude and told me what he would like me to do. I helped sort out some of the papers for the lads who had arrived and then popped out to deliver a round myself. After that I told him to give me a ring whenever he got stuck. He paid me well for my trouble and it did not impinge on my 'proper' job.

Being on his own, working seven days a week, and having developed his business over quite some years, Charlie had never taken a holiday. He was in desperate need of a break, so it was that one day he asked me whether I would be willing to give up a week of my annual leave from work to run the shop for him whilst he took a vacation. In exchange, he offered to pay me the equivalent of what I was earning in one month at the hospital. As he had no-one else to turn to and his offer was very attractive, I agreed to do it, although I was very nervous about being left with such a responsibility and no-one to refer to should I meet with a problem. However, it all went very smoothly and he was more than pleased with what he found when he got back.

One morning he called me to help him and I responded immediately, missing my breakfast to do so. On leaving his shop he asked if I could help again the following day. I agreed. But the following morning, I had hardly stepped into his shop when he let out a flood of anger and bad language at me. I had made a mistake in sorting out the papers for one of the rounds the previous morning, and my error had resulted in a domino effect whereby he had apparently received a number calls from infuriated customers complaining at having received the wrong newspaper. With all the boys having finished their rounds and gone home, he had had to go out himself and spend a few hours sorting it out.

I apologised and apologised, but his anger was relentless. He called me an idiot, an imbecile, stupid. Even as I got on with sorting out the papers into the various rounds before the boys arrived, he kept firing another shot at me. I could not wait to get out of the shop. I was so angry and upset at this unexpected barrage of abuse. After putting up with it for half an hour I was able to leave the shop to deliver a round in the absence of a boy who had failed to turn up that morning. As I ran from door to door delivering the papers, I decided that Charlie clearly needed to be taught a lesson; that he was not to talk to me like that ever again. I decided that I would never step inside that shop again until he apologised. He needed me more than I needed him … or so I thought!

Thus it was that I avoided the shop like the plague. I also refused to answer the phone, telling my parents that if he rang they were to tell him that I wasn't available to help him.

'I'll make him sweat,' I foolishly thought.

I cut him off completely. My parents had their daily newspaper delivered from Charlie's shop and as I wasn't prepared to enter it, my mother would now have to go there to pay for the papers herself instead of giving the money to me to do it. Whenever she went to the shop Charlie would ask after me and comment on the fact that he had not seen me and send me greetings through my mother. But stubbornly I refused to respond. Days turned into weeks. If my mother wanted anything from his shop, I would cycle a further mile away to get it, rather than walk the few yards from our home and enter that place. I was not going to enter his shop again, not until he came and apologised to me. As far as I was concerned that was that.

Quite a bit of time had passed and I had adjusted to the fact of never ever going into that shop again when my mother came into the lounge where I was sitting one day and announced, 'Charlie's coming up the garden path.' My heart almost jumped into my mouth. 'I bet he's come to see you, do you want to see him?'

'Yes, I replied, 'let him in.'

'At last,' I thought, 'he's come to apologise, I knew he would. I bet he needs my help.'

The bell rang and I heard my mum open the door. They shared a few words on the doorstep before she ushered him into the room, asking him, as she left, if he would like a cup of tea. He said he would and she then shut the door. He sat down in the armchair opposite me and we looked at each other across the room in silence for quite some time.

'So what's the matter?' he asked, breaking the uncomfortable silence.

'What do you mean, what's the matter?' I replied.

'Well, I haven't seen you for months and you haven't been in the shop or able to help me out and I wondered what the matter was?' he said.

'You know what the matter is,' I then retorted.

'No, I don't. You tell me,' he responded.

My mother knocked on the door at this point and brought us each a cup of tea. 'I hope it's all right and how you like it,' she said.

'It's perfect, Mrs Webber,' he replied.

'Well,' I started as mum left the room, 'you know how hard I have worked for you and how willing I have always been to help you out. I know you pay me well but it isn't all about money. I'd probably help you out for nothing if you were stuck. You have called on me in all weathers; sometimes it has not been at all convenient. Often with the lateness of your call I have had to go without my breakfast or else

I would have been late for work, but did I ever complain? No, yet I make one mistake – and yes there were some unfortunate consequences – and you rip me to shreds. You tear me to pieces with your tongue lashing. And even though I apologised several times, you just would not let it go, would you? After all I have done for you I really didn't deserve that humiliation in front of the boys and the customers who came in that morning!'

I stopped and he sat staring at me in silence as I awaited his response. It was a long time coming.

'Have you finished?' he begun.

'Yes,' I replied.

'You know your trouble, don't you?' He waited, but his response had caught me off guard. I didn't know quite what to say in reply. So he repeated himself. 'You know your trouble don't you? You're obsessed with yourself. All you ever think about is *you*.' I was flabbergasted. This was not what I expected. I was indignant as I stopped him in his tracks.

'What do you mean, I'm obsessed with myself? All I ever think about is me? I'm always thinking of other people. Not only have I helped you every time you have wanted me, I'm always helping other people. You ask my mum. If ever she needs my help I'm always willing. And if I see things to be done, I don't wait to be asked. For years now, even when I was at school, I have visited my gran at the other end of the city and done jobs for her every Saturday morning, shopping, gardening, chopping logs, all sorts of things.' So it was that I continued to wax lyrical about my good deeds, expecting him to be surprised at what he heard and convinced that he was wrong. He just sat there in silence, taking it all in; waiting until I had exhausted my shopping list.

There followed another long silence before Charlie then said, 'See what I mean? All you think about is you. "I do this, I do that. Look at me, aren't I a hero? Aren't I good?" All I can hear is, "Me, me, me, me." You need to hear yourself, Howard.'

I was speechless. He then looked at his watch and said, 'Well I've got lots to do and can't sit listening to this all day.' Getting up from his seat he added, 'When you've sorted yourself out come and see me,' adding, 'I'll let myself out,' as he opened the lounge door and was gone.

I sat there stunned. This was not how it was meant to be. There had not been even a hint of regret or contrition, never mind the remotest sign of the apology that I had anticipated. In fact he had added even more fuel to the fire of anger and resentment that burned within me. He had come round to my home and added even more insult to the injury he inflicted when last we met. How dare he say such a thing? I was livid. I was fuming. It was as if he had come and ripped off the scab from a wound whose pain had given way to sore-ness and had, to some degree, been gradually healing, only to be made to bleed all over again. Only this time it was an even worse bleed.

For the next few days all I could think of was that encounter and my foolishness in being totally unprepared for what happened. I had never considered any other possible outcome from us meeting again other than an expression of regret on his part for the unjust and totally uncalled for way he had treated me that morning all those weeks earlier. I mulled it over and over in my mind for days. It af-fected my sleep as I lay in bed thinking up scenario after scenario in my search for a way whereby I might hurt him as much as he had hurt me … but I couldn't find one that would do the trick. It all achieved me nothing and the lack of sleep began to have a bad effect on my health.

I knew my mother didn't like the man and was pleased that I was no longer associating with him, but although I found his coarse-ness offensive, he had been very kind and generous to me and shown a special trust in me. Also, he wasn't a man without virtue. He was honest. He was reliable. He kept his word. Any promises he made he stood by. He didn't suffer fools gladly, and was adept at 'reading' people, probably the result of his many years as a regimental sergeant-major. Though not educated in the conventional sense, he was very knowledgeable and well-read. Many had been the occasion that he would invite me to his flat for a few hours in the evening, where we would share food and have some deep discussion about religion, faith, God, or politics. Sometimes he would tell me about his experiences at Arnhem in 1944, or later in Palestine and then during the Suez Crisis. I had considered him my friend.

Following that unexpected second verbal assault, time passed and I thought more deeply and questioningly about what he had said when he came to my home. What if he was right? Maybe I did think more highly of myself than I should? Maybe even any good I ever did *was* really all about me, me, me? As I continued to ponder over it all I came to the conclusion that what Charlie had done was puncture my pride. Maybe he should not have reacted as he did. Perhaps his response to that one single error was totally unreasonable, but it wasn't something new that I hadn't seen happen before. I had witnessed him 'lose it' with others on a number of occasions through the years. On those occasions I had stood idly by and done nothing. Despite what I told myself, my response to his explosion of anger towards me really had little to do with the rights or wrongs of what he said, but rather the hurt I felt. Had it been about justice, surely I would have leapt to the defence of one of the other lads when, from time to time, Charlie had let them have 'both barrels' so to speak? Whilst I pitied the victim of his diatribe, I never once said a word to chastise Charlie for his behaviour. Yet how different my response had been when I was on the receiving end.

Another issue also arose in my mind. I claimed to be a Christian, albeit a very immature one. He knew what I claimed. We had discussed our views on the subject. Where, I now asked myself, was there any sign of forgiveness in the way I had responded to him? What message was I sending to him? One thing that was clear about Charlie was that he never held a grudge. Once he had expressed himself clearly and got it all off his chest, (OK, maybe using diabolical language), that was the end of it. In this aspect he showed himself to be a far better man than I, and that was not his only virtue. So it was that I eventually came to the conclusion that I needed to let bygones be bygones and swallow what I now knew to be my pride and pray for the courage to enter his shop again.

It sounds pretty pathetic, but although I didn't want or need it, I decided to pop in to the shop on my way home from work and buy myself a packet of chewing gum. Trying to look bold, like teenagers do when their stomachs are churning, I opened the door. There were no other customers there and Charlie was standing behind the counter with his head down doing some paperwork. He looked up at the sound of my approach,

'Howard, how are you?' he asked, looking most surprised to see me.

'All right,' said I as I lifted a chewing gum packet from the display on the counter in front of me and offered him my money.

'You couldn't look after the shop for half-an-hour, could you? Are you in a hurry? Mrs Cage[13], went home just before a whole load of stuff got delivered. The lorry driver unloaded it, but it's all standing on the floor in the back room waiting to be put away in the store. I can't do that and serve in the shop at the same time. Would you help me?' he asked.

'Of course,' I said, as someone entered the shop behind me.

'Hello, Howard,' said the older man who had just come in from a torrential downpour outside. I made my way round to the other side of the counter as Charlie vanished into the back room. Shaking his umbrella the man added, 'long time - no see; I've missed seeing you about.'

And that is how that episode ended. Charlie never ever broached the subject of my dispute with him or my reaction to his verbal attack on me all those months earlier. Neither did he mention

---

[13]   His part-time assistant

again what he said to me when he came to my home and gave me a second helping. He acted as though nothing had ever come between us. I learnt a lot about my pride, something that previously I might have denied having, but there it stopped. It never led me to consider or even think of the concept of my need to die, of dying with Christ. Though the New Testament is saturated with the concept, it would be decades before its truths penetrated my thick skull and my even thicker soul.

Looking back at all these experiences, and looking more deeply at scripture, it was as if the scales began to fall from the eyes of what I now saw to be a rather pathetic disciple. A thing that we fail to notice for years seems blindingly obvious when eventually our eyes are opened to it, and we are left wondering just how could we have missed it?

PART TWO

HOW COULD I HAVE BEEN SO BLIND?

CHAPTER 14

THE DAILY DEATH OF JESUS

It amazes me how, once the Holy Spirit opens our eyes to something we were previously blind to, we see illustrations of our newly discovered truth everywhere. We see what we have never seen before in scripture that we are familiar with, and maybe have read hundreds of times, and wonder how we missed it. It all seems blindingly obvious!

For instance, as I once again read the gospels, I suddenly realised that there is a sense in which Christ Jesus died long before he climbed Calvary's hill. Even in him leaving his heavenly home and becoming a man there is an element of his dying, dying to self, self denial:

> *He left his father's throne above,*
> *So free, so infinite his grace,*
> *Emptied himself of all but love,*
> *And bled for Adam's helpless race.*
> Charles Wesley

Jesus existed before the world began. He has always been the Son of God, and always had God's nature. In John 10:30 he said, 'I and the Father are one,' and again in verses 36-38, he says, '… Why then do you accuse me of blasphemy because I said, "I am God's Son?" Do not believe me unless I do what my Father does. But if I do it, even though you do not believe me, believe the miracles, that you may know and understand that the Father is in me and I in the Father.' Is it little wonder that the religious Jews, who just could not accept his divine claims and credentials despite the evidence of their very own eyes, sought to seize him? (v. 39)

Earlier, (v. 31), when they picked up stones to throw at him and he questioned whether they intended to stone him because of the many great miracles they had witnessed, they replied, 'We are not stoning you for any of these, but for the blasphemy, because you, a mere man, claim to be God' (v. 33).

Jesus is and ever was God. 'By him all things were created: things in heaven and on earth, visible and invisible, … all things were created by him and for him' (Colossians 1:16). Jesus is and ever was God (Philippians 2:6), yet, in Jesus' coming to earth, God made himself nothing (v. 7). He, who was all powerful, all knowing and everywhere present, parted with all of that to confine himself to the limits of a man. He became a human being, a creature, no longer all powerful, all knowing, and everywhere present. He who was totally independent, became dependent. He who was co-equal to the Father in power and glory emptied himself and placed himself in a subservient position to his Father. Although he was still God, he forfeited his kingship for servant-hood and 'did not consider equality with God (his Father), something to be grasped'(v. 6). Therein is that element of self-death. God in Christ Jesus denied himself and exchanged the royal riches of his heavenly home for the poverty of a pauper.

More than that, amazingly he made himself as small and as vulnerable as he could. He could not have been smaller when he entered this world as a tiny baby with his care in the hands of two very poor and inexperienced teenagers. He could have exchanged his heavenly home for the earthly opulence of a palace. Instead, as we read the story of his birth we discover that there was nowhere for him to lay his head. In fact, unlike most people, he was to never have a permanent home, something that even birds and foxes have (Matthew 8:20). No nursery niceties for him, not even the meanest or lowliest of cots. Mary and Joseph had to make do with what they were able find in their temporary abode, an animal's eating trough, a manger (Luke 2:7). Could he have had a lower entry into the world? Could he have been any more vulnerable and dependent?

Yet 'in very nature' (Philippians 2:6) he was still God. The true meaning of the Greek words that St Paul employs, that we translate as 'in very nature God,' conveys the essence of the unchangeable heart of something, the nature of something that always has been and always will be. Yet, as can be seen in his birth and throughout his life, he was also truly and properly man.

Paul shares all of this as an example to us, 'Your attitude should be the same as that of Christ Jesus' (v. 5). In that light, Jesus' words are even more powerful and moving, 'If anyone would come after me,' he said, 'he must deny himself and take up his cross *daily* and follow me. For whoever wants to save his life will lose it, but whoever loses his life for me will save it' (Luke 9:23-24). It seems obvious that to 'come after' him must surely mean that he has gone before; that he has already taken the steps he would have us take. Surely he was taking up his cross daily long before that fateful Friday?

The first followers of Jesus took quite some time to realise what God in Christ had done at his incarnation. St Paul, for instance, wrote his letter to the Philippians sometime after AD 54. His letter to the Colossians was similarly written a considerable time after Christ's return to heaven. An understanding of all that the disciples had experienced in the company of Jesus, and the realisation of exactly who it was that they had walked with, would only begin to dawn on them following Christ's resurrection when they themselves were filled with that self-same Spirit that Jesus had. Indeed, that is what Jesus himself had said, 'But the Counsellor, the Holy Spirit, whom the Father will send in my name, will teach you all things and will remind you of everything I have said to you' (John 14:26). 'But when he, the Spirit of truth, comes, he will guide you into all truth' (John 16:13).

Turning to Christ's life and ministry, right at the start Mark 1:12 tells us that following his baptism, the Holy Spirit 'drove' Jesus into the wilderness (RSV), a verb that the other synoptic gospel writers avoid, preferring to use the tamer verb 'led.' Who, by choice, would leave dizzy spiritual heights for a dark and lonely wilderness? Who would choose to be tried and tested? Jesus had feelings just like you and I, but he was not controlled by those feelings or by his human preferences. Often he did what naturally a person would not be inclined to do simply because it was what the Holy Spirit required/desired. In the wilderness itself, Satan persisted in appealing to areas where Satan frequently has control. But the ploy that succeeded with Adam failed with Jesus. That which was alive in Adam and in us, his descendants, was dead in Jesus. Despite that truth, Satan never gave up trying to awaken it.

We see Satan trying to awaken it using Peter, when Peter took Jesus aside and rebuked him immediately following Jesus telling his disciples about the way he was to suffer and be killed, (Mark 8: 33). Peter meant well. He loved and cared for Jesus. What he said was out of his love and concern for Jesus, but Jesus knew that the source of Peter's remonstration was Satan. Satan is subtle and sly. He will often use a dear friend who loves us and who is concerned for us in his effort to catch us off guard. We, like Peter, often fail to see God's view of a situation and we make our decisions, with the best of intentions, from a human perspective. Satan will always suggest an easier way, a way that we would prefer; an attractive way, a way that seems reasonable, sensible, less painful; a way that appeals to our self-preserving, self-promoting instincts, when on many occasions God may require a very different path, a path that might well appear either foolish or unreasonable. The following are just two examples.

In John 4:1-2, when Jesus learned that it had come to the attention of the Pharisees that he was now 'gaining and baptising' more disciples than John, he left the area. Why did he do that? Should any of us have been found in the same situation, we might well have enjoyed the comparison. Jesus, however, would neither accept or enjoy such comparison. When our success is measured against the sincere but less successful efforts of another, that person is naturally lowered in the eyes of the observer. Jesus was in the business, and is still in the business, of lifting up his humble servants, not having them put down, 'Humble yourselves before the Lord, and he will lift you up' (James 4:10). 'Humble yourselves, therefore, under God's mighty hand, that he may lift you up in due time' (1 Peter 5:6). As Jesus himself said, 'For everyone who exalts himself will be humbled, and he who humbles himself will be exalted, (Luke 14:11). Jesus never exalted himself. He humbled himself and, as a result, his Father exalted him, (Philippians 2:9).

In a second example, Jesus loved his friend Lazarus. 'Yet,' as John 11:6 tells us, 'when he heard that Lazarus was sick, he stayed where he was for two more days.' Why? Was he too busy baptising people? There is no real evidence to support this suggestion. Although John 3:22 records the only reported instance in the gospels of Jesus baptising, later, in John 4:2, we are told that it was not Jesus himself who was doing the baptising, but rather, his disciples.

Others claim that there was no point in Jesus hurrying to Lazarus as he would have been dead by the time Jesus managed to get to him. That may well have been true, but Jesus also loved Mary and Martha so why would he hold back for two whole days from giving them his much needed company and comfort? Had we been in the same position I am sure that we would have dropped everything and gone! Isn't that what good, caring, conscientious Christians do? The difference is that Jesus was not controlled by either his natural human inclinations and feelings, or the pressures, expectations and opinions of others, or indeed by his great compassion, but purely by what the Holy Spirit wanted.

Responding to what the Holy Spirit desired and making his decisions according to the Holy Spirit's dictates was not easy for Jesus. Often such decisions resulted in severe criticism (John 11: 21, 32), and there were times when what the Spirit required troubled him. 'Now my heart is troubled, and what shall I say? Father, save me from this hour? No, it was for this very reason I came to this hour' (John 12:27). Satan was forever throwing alternative and more attractive courses of action into the mind of Jesus. Had it been otherwise the writer of Hebrews 4:15 could hardly have written, '... we have one who has been tempted in every way, just as we are ..'

Dietrich Bonhoeffer said, 'When Christ calls a man, he bids him come and die ... only the man who is dead to his own will can follow Christ. In fact, every command of Jesus is a call to die ... but we do not want to die.'

'I tell you the truth,' said Jesus, 'unless a grain of wheat falls to the ground and dies, it remains only a single seed. But if it dies ...' (John 12:24). If that seed hung on to its life, tried to preserve itself, or looked for somewhere secure and comfortable for itself, it would never fulfill the purpose for which it was created. Only in dying could it truly live, and so too with us. The key to the abundant, fruitful life that Jesus promised, (John 10:10), is death.

It seems to be a key that few find, and those who do eventually find it, often only discover it after a long time of struggle. That promised abundant life seemed to be something that eluded us. We struggled, believing that it was something we received when we achieved, something we might achieve if we managed to climb through a particular hoop. But we could never find the right hoop! We failed to realise that all the hoops we attempted to climb through were hoops of our own making, not God's design. We struggled despite what Jesus taught and revealed in his life and ministry.

I struggled for years to be what God wanted me to be, to

please God. Most times my efforts ended in disappointment and failure. I wanted so much to be 'something' for God. It took me years before I realised that he who 'made himself nothing' (Philippians 2:8), was looking for servants who were willing to be 'nothing' too. Despite my great love for the Lord, I was still the centre of my life, though I couldn't see it and would not have admitted it. My walk with Jesus was all about my effort. It took the words of that very unkind old lady, the words at the beginning of this book, words that wounded me deeply, to bring me to this point of re-evaluation.

I had to admit that I mattered too much to me! It mattered whether I was appreciated, valued, ignored, loved, disliked, overlooked. If I was wronged, I had to rectify it. If someone else got the credit for what I had done, I had to put the record straight. If I got the blame for something that was not my fault, I wasn't willing to accept it as though I was to blame. Yet time and time again I saw in Jesus the complete opposite.

Consider this scene. Fast asleep in the midst of a storm, Jesus was awakened by his disciples with the insulting words, 'Teacher, don't you care if we drown?' (Mark 4:38). Who was in the greater danger, Jesus asleep or the disciples awake? Who were his disciples most concerned about, Jesus or themselves? To say to him, of all people, 'don't you care?' was so insulting. Yet Jesus never reprimanded them for their insult. His rebuke was for their lack of faith.

As another example, at the wedding feast in Cana, someone else got the credit for providing that wonderful wine (John 2:10). The bridegroom who received the accolade deserved condemnation for the near disaster of the wine running out, not praise. Jesus must have heard it all in the open-plan design of that Galilean home, but he never said a word. There is no evidence that he ever put the record straight.

One more illustration of this. On the cross he willingly took the blame, the punishment and shame for sins that he had not committed, as though he was the guilty one. Many who watched that day assumed Jesus was suffering because he deserved it. They were in no doubt that he had offended God.

'... *we considered him stricken by God, smitten by him and afflicted.*
But he was pierced for our transgressions, he was crushed for our iniquities ....'
Isaiah 53:4,5

I discovered that God wasn't wanting my improvement, but rather my removal! In the well known and lovely chorus, 'Let the beauty of Jesus be seen in me,' there is one line that troubles me, 'O thou Spirit divine, all my nature refine.' I think it's wrong! I don't think it's biblical. God does not want to refine this human nature of ours; he wants to replace it, supplant it, to put it to death and replace it with his nature. 'If anyone is in Christ, he is a new creation; the old has gone, the new has come' (2 Corinthians 5:17). My problem was that I was still a caterpillar, albeit a caterpillar who wanted to fly, a caterpillar who was trying to fly, but a caterpillar nevertheless. I discovered that the only way I could fly was for a complete transformation; for that caterpillar to die, to be gone, so that a butterfly could take its place.

It was something St Paul discovered, 'I die every day,' he wrote, hammering the point home, 'I mean that brothers' (2 Corinthians 15:31). A dead corpse has no concern for itself. If you prod it and poke it, insult it or damage it in any way, it will not respond. I realised that Jesus could not possibly begin to truly live his life in me or through me unless I died. The truth is that only Jesus can ever live a life pleasing to God. We have to submit, we have to surrender, we have to give up our control so that our life is no longer our life, but his life. We have to die! 'But we do not want to die,' said Bonhoeffer. How true that is.

Christ's physical death on the cross was essential for our salvation. He died, deserted by those who claimed to love him, condemned by those who didn't. He died alone. And for those who wish to enter that all transforming resurrection life he promised, a life that remains elusive to so many of those who love him, death is the only route. Only in dying do we truly show our trust in God, only in dying do we discover him vindicating his servant, only in dying can Jesus have room to live his life through us, only in dying do we discover the full liberty and release our souls long for. Having said that, our dying must be a daily thing. Why? Because Satan is in the resurrection business too and will always be trying to resurrect the 'old man' in us, as St Paul calls him (Romans 6:6, Ephesians 4:22, Colossians 3:9).

CHAPTER 15

GOOD OR NOT SO GOOD?

There is an assumption that a good child is always the result of good parenting and that a bad child must have had bad or unloving parents. Consequently, there are some wonderful parents who suffer the double agony of firstly, their child turning out to be a delinquent, a drug addict or a social outcast of one sort or another, and secondly, the stigma society attaches to the parents of such children. Such parents are made to feel that they are terrible failures despite the fact that in many an instance they have other children; children who have grown up in the same home and received exactly the same love and attention, who have turned out quite differently to their troubled sibling.

Careless talk from people who have not thought through the issues can wound such a suffering soul deeply. I remember hearing of a very godly church leader, whose son had 'really gone off the rails,' attending a meeting where a more senior church leader was speaking. During his discourse the man spoke of his four children and what wonderful Christians they had turned out to be, and how they were all in Christian ministry of one sort or another. He then went on to say, quite proudly I am sure, that it was the result of the home that they had been brought up in and was a reward from God for their good parenting.

That poor suffering listener went home with the burden he was already carrying, far far heavier. The irrational guilt he felt was not eased, but became almost unbearable. That pious but foolish speaker left that meeting and went home, never to know the untold damage he had done. I imagine he would have been shocked at the very thought that the words of Jesus to the Pharisees could ever have been applied to him, 'Woe to you, because you load people down with burdens they can hardly carry, and you yourselves will not lift one finger to help them' (Luke 11: 46).

Conversely, there are some truly wonderful children who had the worst of starts in life, with selfish, uncaring, unloving, and sometimes quite cruel and neglectful parents, wicked parents. One is always amazed at how such a lovely, caring, hard working and responsible adult could have ever come from such a terrible, dysfunctional home or family. Obviously, there is a greater possibility that good parents will produce good offspring and bad parenting will result in bad offspring. But whilst the probabilities are high in both cases, a good environment is no guarantee of a good result, nor is a bad environment a guarantee of a bad one, as seen in King Hezekiah's case.

Hezekiah, King of Judah (2 Kings chapters 18–20), was the son of a wicked father, Ahaz, and the father of an even more wicked son, Manasseh. But Hezekiah 'did what was right in the eyes of the Lord, just as his father (ancestor) David had done' (2 Kings 18:3). During the very first month of his reign he repaired and opened the doors of the temple in Jerusalem (2 Chronicles 29:3), and within sixteen days he had cleared out all the pagan artefacts from the temple and put back all the objects that had been removed by his father, purifying and consecrating it to God. He then re-established the service of the temple (v. 15-35), and reinstituted the celebration of the Passover (2 Chronicles 30), after which the pagan places of worship were destroyed, sacred stones smashed, and pagan images cut down (2 Chronicles 31:1). Hezekiah even broke the bronze snake that Moses had made (2 Kings 18:4).

By King Hezekiah's time, people were burning incense in honour of that bronze snake, for it had become an object of worship itself. Undoubtedly, one reason that the bronze snake was originally preserved by the nation was that it was a memorial to God's goodness to their forefathers in the wilderness (Numbers 21: 4-9). When the Children of Israel were travelling from Mount Hor to the Red Sea, they got impatient about the situation they were in and they moaned about it. They complained against God and Moses. They complained about the lack of water, the lack of bread and the miserable food they were having to eat. As a result of their rebelliousness and distrust in God, he sent venomous snakes among them.

I often wonder if those venomous snakes were always in close proximity to the people, and whether the people were unaware of the nearby danger simply because God was protecting them by keeping the creatures away from the road on which the Israelites travelled and the places where they camped? I suggest this because I am certain that one day we will discover that God did far more than we ever realised in protecting us from harm. Whilst we may be aware of many instances of his providential care, there are even more instances of us being saved from dangers that we didn't know that we were in. When we were little children and a parent held our hand and took us across a very busy road, did any of us really have any idea of the danger we would have been in had they not been taking care of us?

In response to their complaints about God's care and provision, the Lord let the people have a taste of what it was to have it removed, and let the snakes loose among them. As a consequence, many people were bitten and died from their bites. In desperation people came to Moses and confessed their lack of faith and sinfulness and pleaded with him to speak to God on their behalf. In response to their pleas Moses did just that and God responded to his prayers by telling him to make a snake and put it on a pole so that anyone bitten could look at it and live.

Another reason that they may well have kept that bronze snake was that not only did Moses make it, but God himself had ordered its making. Sadly, those things that God provides to help us with our worship, to increase our understanding of him, or to aid us in remembering his goodness, can so easily and unconsciously be elevated to a status that God never intended for them. How easily those who refuse to worship the images borrowed from the heathen are drawn to deifying symbols, ceremonies, and even people that God may well have ordained, things which in the past have been wonderful instruments of good.

For his part, Hezekiah could have simply forbidden the worship of the bronze snake. It would have been a much easier thing to have done. But the danger of the people returning to worshipping what was essentially 'a piece of brass' (the meaning of the name Nehushtan), would have remained; so he smashed it to pieces. That was a courageous thing to do, even for a king.

There is nothing in Scripture that says that Hezekiah did not appreciate what God had done in the past in using that object, nor that he didn't have some nostalgic or sentimental attachment to it himself. He may well have done so. It was part of the nation's heritage. But Hezekiah believed that the only way to stop it from being misused was to destroy it. He felt that the issues and danger were that serious. Doing what he did never removed from it the important part it had played historically in God's dealings with Israel, nor yet its connection to Christ's saving work which would later be revealed (John 3:14). Just as the image of a venomous snake was put on a pole so that anyone bitten could look at it and live, so too 'God made him who had no sin to be sin for us' (2 Corinthians 5:21) and had him nailed to a cross, so that anyone stricken and afflicted by sin could look on him hanging there, with the appearance of a sinner, and live.

Sometimes, as with Hezekiah, we have to act in controversial ways that we and maybe others find painful and upsetting, for there are things that need to be done, need to be said, and need to be written if we are to progress along God's planned pathway. Some seem more concerned at preserving the ashes of past fires than having a living fire burning in their midst like their forefathers once knew. Today, there seems to be an absence of that passion and willingness to do anything, sacrifice anything, (however dear to us), combined with a willingness to remove everything that prevents God giving to them that all-consuming, inextinguishable blaze. '... let us throw off everything that hinders and the sin that so easily entangles ...' is the call of Hebrews 12:1. We are ever in danger of our helps becoming our hindrances, his past channels becoming our present obstacles.

But what, in the context of this book, is the reason that we have turned our attention to Hezekiah? In 2 Kings 18:5-6 we read, 'Hezekiah trusted in the Lord, the God of Israel.' There was no-one like him among the kings of Judah, either before him or after him. He held fast to the Lord and did not cease to follow him; he kept the commands the Lord had given Moses. What a wonderful testimony. Yet, Hezekiah was not without difficulties and failings, both personal and national in nature.

During his reign the Assyrians invaded the northern Kingdom of Israel, and its capital, Samaria, fell. Hezekiah had rebelled against the Assyrian king, Sennacherib, and so the Assyrian king's attention now turned towards Judah, the southern kingdom. Having first attacked and conquered the fortified cities of Judah, Sennacherib then threatened Jerusalem itself. In desperation King Hezekiah went to the Temple (2 Kings 19:1) and sent his servant to request that Isaiah pray about the situation (v. 2-4). Hezekiah knew that his forces were no match against the Assyrian army ... and so did Sennacherib! The result of Isaiah's prayers was a temporary respite which was then followed by yet another threat, (v. 9-13). Ultimately, following the mysterious deaths of 185,000 soldiers in the Assyrian camp, there was a total withdrawal without a single arrow being fired. Sennacherib returned home to Ninevah, but one day, while worshipping in the temple of his god, he was murdered by two of his own sons (v. 35-37).

Around the same time, Hezekiah was taken ill, so ill that he almost died. The pastoral visit he received from Isaiah was no comfort at all. Any joy he might have felt in the visit, with the prophet finding time and being good enough to call, soon evaporated as Isaiah told him, 'This is what the Lord says: Put your house in order, because you are going to die; you will not recover' (2 Kings 20: 1). I wonder whether any of us would want Isaiah to be our minister, our pastoral visitor? Like so many good, godly people who receive similar personal bad news, Hezekiah was confused and upset. He turned his face to the wall and prayed his heart out, reminding God of his faithfulness and wholehearted devotion, whilst weeping bitterly. And God responded to his cries immediately (v4). It is indeed wonderful to receive an immediate response to our heart cries.

As Peter sunk beneath the waves, having stepped out of the boat to walk to Jesus and then looked away from Jesus to the fury of the wind and waves about him, he cried, 'Lord, save me.' His prayer could not have been shorter but Christ's response could not have been quicker. 'Immediately, Jesus reached out his hand and caught him' (John 14:29-31). George Muller, that great man of prayer of the 19th century knew immediate answers to his prayers, but he also knew what it was to pray daily, with decades passing before seeing an answer. If there is a delay in God answering our cries, we are in good company. Like Muller, we need to persevere. In this instance, Isaiah hadn't even left the palace grounds when God sent him back to Hezekiah with the reassuring words that God had heard his cries and would heal him and give him another fifteen years of life. He also assured him that he would defend the city from the Assyrians.

The King of Babylonia had heard of Hezekiah's illness, and sent messengers with a letter and a gift to him as he recovered (2

Kings 20: 12). At that time Babylonia was not a significant player on the world stage, though it did have aspirations. Like the people of Judah, the Babylonians lived under the constant threat of the Assyrians. One day Babylonia would take over and enlarge the Assyrian Empire, but at that time there was no way that Hezekiah could ever have imagined Babylonia becoming a threat to Judah. Who, in the early 1920s, could ever have imagined that the little ex-painter and decorator with the funny moustache and grandiose political ambitions would ever become a threat to the whole civilised world? How often do any of us recognise the significance of small things, the innocuous vehicles by which Satan, in Trojan Horse fashion, commences the work that will result in him reigning in the human heart?

'Hezekiah had very great riches and honour, and he made treasuries for his silver and gold and precious stones, spices, shields and all kinds of valuables ... for God had given him very great riches' (2 Chronicles 32:27-29). When these Babylonian messengers arrived, Hezekiah was totally open and trusting of them and gave them a guided tour of his palace and storerooms, showing them his silver and gold, perfumes and spices. There was nothing in either his storerooms or his kingdom that he did not show them. He even showed them his military equipment (2 Kings 20:13). It's a bit like showing a potential burglar round our home, pointing out all the things of value that we have and what our security is like. Basically, Hezekiah was showing off. It was all about Hezekiah's pride. He never introduced them to Isaiah and Isaiah was never told of their visit. Nevertheless, Isaiah did get to know of it.

'What did those men say, and where did they come from' (v. 14), Isaiah eventually asked, and 'What did they see in your palace?' (v. 15).

God had miraculously saved Hezekiah twice; once, when the Assyrians threatened Jerusalem and a second time, when he was seriously ill. However, when the king of Babylon's messengers arrived immediately following his recovery, having heard of the miracle that

God had performed, (2 Chronicles 32:31), there is no evidence that Hezekiah took them around the House of God, the Temple. Nor does it appear that he told them about the One who had miraculously saved him. No! What we are told is that he showed them round his palace. He showed off his possessions, his accumulated material wealth. They were pagan messengers, idol worshippers, probably totally unfamiliar with Israel's God. The only reason they visited Hezekiah was because of his miraculous healing. One surely would have thought that he would have impressed upon them something of the holiness and power of Israel's God? But we see no mention of it in either of the accounts[14] of their visit.

Having received their gift and greeting, Hezekiah was more concerned about showing off that which he had acquired rather than telling them of that which God had done for him. This self interest and self concern is confirmed when Isaiah chastises him for his foolishness, telling him that one day the Babylonians would take away everything from his palace, and including his own descendants.

And what was Hezekiah's response? Was it prayers and pleading? Tears? Concern for what would happen to his people, indeed for his family? No. He was just relieved to know that none of it would happen in his lifetime ... 'The word of the Lord you have spoken is good,' Hezekiah replied to Isaiah. 'Will there not be peace and security in my lifetime?' he thought (v. 19). The Bible makes it clear that Hezekiah was a particularly good king, but as good and sincere as he was, Hezekiah's main concern was for himself. He still considered everything in relation to himself. The 'old man' in Hezekiah, the Adam in him had not been crucified.

Hezekiah loved God but it was a lesser love than he had for himself. For all he had done for God, his heart wasn't in tune with God. Many an otherwise good man suffers from the same sin. With the years it is so easy to gradually become proud of one's position,

---

14   As well as the account of the Babylonians envoys in 1 Kings 20:12-19, the story is also told in Isaiah 39:1-8.

one's standing, one's virtues, what we seem to have achieved. In the story of the prodigal son that Jesus tells, the son who remained at home with his father was a good man. He had stuck close to his father and worked hard after his younger brother deserted the family home and went away and wasted his inheritance. He never made unreasonable demands. No one could call him a 'waster.' But sadly, we can see how he developed an inflated view of his own goodness and lacked the heart of the father he served (Luke 15:25ff). He lacked all humility and thought himself superior to his brother, obviously preoccupied with his own importance. I fear that was my bandmaster's problem.

What a contrast there is between the attitude of Hezekiah and that of Jesus. When Jesus looked upon the city of Jerusalem he wept (Luke 19:41-44), even though the destruction he foretold for it would not occur for another thirty-seven years, well after he had ascended into heaven. Whilst Hezekiah was quick to plead for his own life when he was told that he would die of his illness, there was no apparent pleading that God might relent from fulfilling what he had predicted for the nation. So different too was he to Moses, following the sin of his people and the impending punishment that awaited them, 'O what a great sin these people have committed,' he said, 'they have made themselves gods of gold. But now,' he pleaded, 'please forgive their sin – but if not, then blot me out of the book you have written' (Exodus 32:31-32).

CHAPTER 16

FORESHADOW OF CHRIST?

Most of us prefer comfort to discomfort, ease rather than difficulties, and peace rather than conflict. We will go out of our way to avoid any sort of unpleasantness, anything that would upset our equilibrium. Nehemiah knew security, comfort, prestige and position in the palace of Artexerxes, Emperor of Persia. He also seems to have lived happily with the delusion that all was well back in Jerusalem. Ignorance can indeed be bliss.

Forty-nine years after the destruction of Jerusalem in 587 BC, King Cyrus issued a decree ordering the restoration of the Jewish community and religion in Jerusalem. He allowed the Jews who had been exiled to Babylon to return to that city and rebuild the temple there, and even authorised that the expenses be paid from the royal treasury, providing Cyrus with a say in how the temple was to be built. In addition, he returned the sacred vessels that Nebuchadnezzar, the Babylonian King, had removed from the temple (Ezra 6:3-5). All this took place in 538 BC, the year after Cyrus, King of Persia, had conquered the Babylonians. His policy regarding conquered and exiled people was very different to the Babylonian king, whose empire he inherited. It was a policy of repatriation.

As a consequence, a group of the exiled Jews returned from Babylon, full of enthusiasm at the thought of rebuilding the temple and the nation, believing that it was the beginning of a wonderful new episode, a new beginning brought about by God. The contingent, however, seems to have been quite small in number which was hardly surprising. Jerusalem was far away and only the oldest people would have remembered life there. The journey would have been a difficult and dangerous one, and even with the promise of support from King Cyrus, the task ahead was a daunting one with the prospects of success uncertain. Also, many of the Jews who had been born in Babylon were well settled and prospering there. Whilst most may have been willing to support the venture financially (Ezra 1:4,6), Josephus, the Jewish historian records that they were 'not willing to leave their possessions.'

The foundations of the temple were laid in that first wave of enthusiasm, although not without difficulty. There was opposition to the new arrivals from those already living in the area and hostility from the neighbouring Samaritan governor. Various disappointments, frustrations and discouragements year on year took their toll on the people. Although further groups followed that initial party, the numbers returning from exile remained small. A succession of poor seasons and partial crop failures left many with inadequate food and clothing. They were in a far worse state than they would have been had they stayed in Babylon. Eighteen years after that initial positive optimistic start, the rebuilding of the temple had progressed no further than the foundations.

In 520 BC, the prophets Haggai and Zechariah arrived on the scene, and their very positive message was the catalyst needed to re-invigorate the people with new hope. The project was restarted and within five years the temple was completed. Those Jews involved in its rebuilding believed that it would herald the re-establishment of David's throne and a new messianic age for the nation. However,

142

when that did not materialise, any hope the people had of a golden future evaporated and any further plans to restore the rest of the city, most of which was still in ruins, ended.

Seventy years after the completion of the temple, Nehemiah received a visit from his brother Hanani and some other men who had returned from Judah. When Nehemiah heard about what was happening back in his homeland he was shocked. Hanani told of how the people who had returned were living in disgrace and in great trouble, and how the walls of the city were still broken down and the gates burned. Over one hundred and forty years had passed since the city's destruction and it was now over ninety years since the first exiles returned. Nehemiah just sat down and wept (Nehemiah 1:1-4).

How is it that the news came as such a shock to Nehemiah? He obviously assumed that all was going well back in Jerusalem. Maybe those in the palace only knew what those in charge of the West Euphrates Province[15] wanted them to know. What province governor would tell the emperor everything, especially when it might reflect badly on his governorship? Perhaps Nehemiah was so busy getting on with his own life that he gave little thought to what was happening so far away. None of it had anything to do with where he was and what he was doing. Out of sight, out of mind is not an uncommon human trait.

The news, when it came, was like a bombshell. For some days Nehemiah mourned and could not eat. But what could he do? In his helplessness and powerlessness he presented it all to God. Neither his elevated position and personal security, nor his material comforts, could take away the pain that discovering the needs and demise of his fellow Jews brought him. Unlike King Hezekiah, he could not sit back smugly, pleased that it wasn't happening to him, just relieved that he wasn't in the same unfortunate position. He could have praised and thanked God that he was far removed from it all ... but

---

[15]   Under Persian rule Judah was part of this large province west of the River Euphrates.

he didn't. In contrast to Hezekiah, he took no pleasure in the fact that he personally was not a victim, and four months later we find him still miserable.

Obviously Nehemiah did not wear his heart on his sleeve. He had a job to do. He was the cup-bearer of King Artaxerxes,(v 11), a later successor of King Cyrus. It was Nehemiah's job to taste the wine before the king drank it as a test of its acceptability. It was not unknown in the ancient world for an assassin to provide a king with a poisoned chalice. Thus, though he was daily in the presence of the king, Artaxerxes never saw through the untroubled veneer, the façade, the mask Nehemiah wore in public. How slow the king was to realise his unhappiness. Obviously, a king would have many important matters of state to deal with, serious problems to attend to, leaders to be addressed, foreign emissaries to be received. He probably paid little attention to his cup-bearer standing in the wings, awaiting his next request.

It is easy to be so preoccupied with what we are doing, even things we are doing in the service of God, that we fail to pay any real attention to the people we meet or regularly have dealings with. We don't discern their need or the distress hidden behind a smiling face because they never have our full interest and attention. Our minds are always elsewhere. We can so easily allow the task at hand to become more important than people, ordinary people. For some of us, a thing has to be blindingly obvious, spelt out in capital letters, before we ever notice it, and even then we do not always cotton on.

I'm reminded of a very caring godly minister who was planning a conference at his church and working out the train times for the guest speaker. He had an urgent need to complete the task by the end of the day, but still had a number of telephone calls to make. One call he made, which he thought was to the railway travel enquiries, was answered by what was obviously an elderly lady. Realising that he had got a wrong number he apologised profusely to the old lady who replied, 'That is all right. I've been on my own all day and

144

have not seen or heard from anyone for almost a week. When the telephone rang I thought it was a friend phoning me. I thought I was going to have someone to talk to.'

'I'm so sorry to disappoint you,' the minister answered before hurriedly wishing the woman well and, with a 'God bless you,' placing the telephone back on the receiver.

Again he picked up the phone and this time was relieved to find that he had rung the right number. By the end of the day, he managed to complete all that needed to be done and, satisfied that all his plans were in place for a successful conference, went off to bed. Only as he lay in bed thinking of the various things that had taken place that day, did his mind return to that old lady that he had inadvertently phoned that afternoon. As he thought of what she had said, he suddenly realised what an opportunity he had missed. It was clear from her few words that she was lonely, in need of company, in need of some contact with a fellow human being, and he had been so preoccupied and insensitive as to hardly give her the time of day. The following thought also entered his mind. 'God himself could well have created this opportunity for me to be an answer to her prayers and a blessing to her, but I was so preoccupied with "me" and the task I had set myself that I hardly paid any attention to her and her obvious need. A conversation with her may have only taken five or ten minutes out of my day, but it may have made a world of difference to her week'

Some things that we get wrong can be corrected. In this case, with no record of the number that he had accidentally dialled, he could never get back to the lady and have that conversation. However, the saving grace was that the incident changed him. He became more attentive to others, more people focused and less task orientated.

One day, whilst on duty, Nehemiah let the veil slip sufficiently for the king to notice sorrow in Nehemiah's face and he enquired as to the reason for his sad demeanour, so Nehemiah told him.

'What is it you want?' the king then asked him. What a question! It is one thing to know a problem, but quite another to know what to do about it so, immediately before answering, Nehemiah prayed. It cannot have been a very long prayer. Now have you ever said something and even as you are speaking wondered why you are saying what you are saying? Have you ever thought that what you are saying sounds ridiculous, even as you are saying it? I shared a personal experience of that in an earlier chapter. There is no evidence of Nehemiah ever having had any building experience, so what on earth possessed him to say, 'If it pleases the king and if your servant has found favour in his sight, let him send me to the city in Judah where my fathers are buried so that I can rebuild it'? (2:5). Surely, such a response could only have been made under the Holy Spirit's diretion?

Nehemiah did not know what would await him in Jerusalem and whether or not he would be accepted or could do what needed to be done. He was a successful and much appreciated cup-bearer, but builder? Organiser? Leader? He could have been a complete and utter failure, yet he was willing to give up his prestigious position in a palace for a building site and a group of discouraged, disheartened, disillusioned people. The reason? Because, most probably as a result of his prayer, something within convicted him of the course he must take, and as a result, he trusted God to help him. Also, he loved the people. How often does God's way appear utter foolishness and destined to end in failure?

To those who will bravely give up all to venture forth for God; to willingly build that which has collapsed, fallen, or been taken by the enemy, Satan will always have a reception committee waiting to ensure that they have a rough time. It was no different for Nehemiah. Things would have been hard enough without opposition, but Sanballat, who we know was the governor of the province of Samaria[16] was angry and incensed (4:1). He, with the support of Tobiah the Ammonite, (v. 3), would do all he could to obstruct Nehemiah and

---

[16]   We know this from the Elephantine papyri.

discourage the people from supporting him. Why did they take such a stance? In his autobiographical book, Nehemiah tells us in chapter 2:10 that it was because, 'someone had come to promote the welfare of the Israelites.' Satan has a habit of planting a Sanballat or Tobiah in a congregation, someone or more than one, who will do all they can to obstruct God's plans and make things difficult for those who truly belong to him.

One is reminded of the anger and violent opposition in Birmingham, Alabama to another prophet, Dr Martin Luther King, who 'had come to promote the welfare' of his people. The Commissioner for Public Safety in the city, 'Bull' Connor, showed a willingness to use violence, even against children, when 2,500 black children marched in protest against the city's unjust segregation laws in May 1963. He had fire hoses turned on them that had such power as to sweep them off their feet and tear their clothes off their backs, before then letting dogs loose among them. In the chaos at least three children were badly bitten. But demonstration after demonstration continued even though the non-violence of these demonstrations was continually met with fire hoses, dogs and even armoured cars.

One cannot read the words Martin Luther King, Jr. chose to rouse the nation without sensing something of the Spirit of Jesus as well as obedience to Christ's command that we love our enemies (Matthew 5:44), in that speech:

> *We must say to our white brothers all over the south who try to keep us down: 'We will match your capacity to inflict suffering with our capacity to endure it. We will meet your physical force with our soul force. We will not hate you. And yet we cannot in all good conscience obey your evil laws. Do to us what you will. Threaten our children and we will still love you ... Say that we're too low, that we're too degraded, yet we will still love you ... Bomb our homes and ... our churches ... and we will still love you.'*

147

Despite all the odds stacked against Nehemiah, he seems to have kept a sound head on his shoulders. Aware of the enormity of the task and his lack of resources, he enlisted the help of King Artaxerxes who released him from his royal duties, provided him with safe passage (Nehemiah 2:7), and supplied him with all the timber required from his own forest (v. 8). On arrival in Jerusalem, Nehemiah waited three days before he did anything and even then made his first job that of a reconnaissance of the city at night.

He wisely made his own assessment of the situation, supplementing what others had told him with a firsthand investigation of his own. He confided in no man what God had inspired him to do (2:12). He took only a few companions with him on his trip around the city at night. Away from public gaze they would see what he saw and see it as he saw it. One sees something of the same intimacy in the relationship of Jesus with his disciples in his approach.

The task was an impossible one; Nehemiah would not have got as far as having an interview had he come with his credentials to you or me for the job. It was a foolhardy, reckless, ridiculous venture for Nehemiah to set out on, even without Sanballat and Tobiah's interfering. At the outset God's plans often seem absurd, ask the likes of Abraham, Moses, Isaiah, or more recently Gladys Aylward, Eric Liddell, David Wilkerson, Jackie Pullinger et al. But those who accept his way find a wonderful equipping-and-providing-God as surely as Nehemiah did.

One cannot help but see so much of the self-denying Christ in Nehemiah, as he weeps over Jerusalem (Nehemiah 1:4), as he takes upon himself the sins of others (1:6), as he gives up his elevated position in a royal palace to share the lot of the common people in their struggles and suffering. Nehemiah built a city's walls whilst Jesus builds a kingdom. Like Jesus, Nehemiah experienced ridicule and mockery (4:1-2), he gave up his rights and privileges, (5:14-15), he comforted the distressed, (4:14), he denounced leaders and officials who burdened the common people, (5:6), he fed those who came to him, (5:17-18), was lied about, (6:5-8), and cancelled the debts of those indebted to him (5:11).

Like Nehemiah's mission, Christ's mission was foolhardy, reckless and ridiculous.

> *'He had no beauty or majesty to attract us to him,*
> *nothing in his appearance that we should desire him.*
> *He was despised and rejected by men,*
> *a man of sorrows , and familiar with suffering*
> *Like one from whom men hide their faces*
> *he was despised , and we esteemed him not.'*
> Isaiah 53:2-3

Many would wish to share his throne, few there are who would wish to share his cross. Many hanker to be noticed, to be bathed in glory. Few there are who will accept the obscurity and ignominy of Calvary, which makes the words of Jesus even more challenging, 'Anyone who does not carry his cross and follow me cannot be my disciple' (Luke 14:27).

CHAPTER 17

LEAST BY CHOICE

To have the most menial task, the most lowly position in the service of God is a privilege beyond anything this world can ever offer. 'Better is one day in your courts than a thousand elsewhere. I would rather be a doorkeeper in the house of my God than dwell in the tents of the wicked' (Psalm 84:10). Far better to be a beggar at God's door, a porter in God's employ, than a prince at the centre of an ungodly palace. Better to have the leftovers when others have eaten their fill from the Master's table (Matthew 15:27), than to sit at a table, however sumptuous the spread, and eat food that will not last (John 6:27). 'Do not love the world or anything in the world. If anyone loves the world, the love of the Father is not in him. For everything in the world – the cravings of sinful man, the lust of his eyes and the boastings of what he has or does – comes not from the Father but from the world' (1 John 2:15-16).

We look back on St Paul as the greatest teacher, evangelist and missionary of all time; someone on whom God relied so much in terms of extending his Kingdom on earth. But it wasn't always like this. Today he is much revered throughout the church worldwide and the letters he sent to a number of churches and individuals are now incorporated into Holy Scripture. His pronouncements on various issues and subjects within those letters have been accepted as God's definitive word. Surely Paul could have never imagined in his wildest dreams how God was going to use his ministry and his writings. How different from what is almost a universal acceptance and adulation of today, was his experience and life back then.

His new life in Christ began in an atmosphere of suspicion, (Acts 9:26), and reading his letters one meets with a lonely man always under attack both from outside that early church and tragically from within its ranks too. Often it was those with power and influence who were among his most hostile adversaries, including some of his fellow preachers who took the opportunity to 'stir up trouble' when Paul found himself in prison. Unlike Paul, they did not preach from pure motives but were motivated by selfish ambition, (Philippians 1:17).

Also there were so called 'super apostles' with an elevated view of themselves. Though trained and quite eloquent in their oratory, they preached a different gospel than Paul did. Obviously, they were highly regarded and accepted by many, hence Paul's nickname for them. Paul wasn't among their number. 'I do not think I am in the least inferior to those "super-apostles." I may not be a trained speaker, but I do have knowledge' (2 Corinthians 11:5-6), and again, 'I am not in the least inferior to the "super-apostles", even though I am nothing' (2 Corinthians 12:11).

Paul's was a life of hardship, loneliness and suffering. When he planted the church in Corinth, he was so beset with difficulties that God had to come in a vision and reassure and encourage him (Acts 18:9). Surely God would not have had to tell Paul not to be afraid if he had not been afraid? To keep on speaking had he not considered stopping? Or even not to give up, (GNV), unless there had been a very real likelihood that he may have done so? What pain it must have caused him later to discover that, after all his time and effort, teaching and suffering, there were things going on amongst what were meant to be God's people in Corinth that even the pagans would not be found doing! (1 Corinthians 5:1).

When we arrive at his final letter to his young friend Timothy, we see there a catalogue of agonies added to his imprisonment and chains. He writes that *everyone* in the province of Asia[17] had deserted him including Phygelus and Hermogenes. We don't know who these two characters were, but the fact that Paul named them means that Timothy knew them and that they would have been the least likely to have left him. One can imagine Paul saying, 'Yes, Timothy, even them!'

Hymenaus and Philetus had 'wandered away from the truth.' They were part of a group of false teachers whose 'teaching,' Paul said, 'will spread like gangrene' (2:17 -18). They may have wandered from the truth but there is no evidence that they had left the church. One can leave the way of truth, not only theologically but also in our spirit, our attitude, and our behaviour, yet still retain membership or a position in the church. Paul also spoke of terrible times coming when 'people will be lovers of themselves, lovers of money, boastful, proud, abusive, disobedient to their parents, ungrateful, unholy, without love, unforgiving, slanderous, without self-control, brutal, not lovers of the good, treacherous, rash, conceited, lovers of pleasure rather than God – having a form of godliness but denying its power' (3:1-5).

The church will always have enemies and slanderers outside its ranks. What some fail to realise is that it will also always have both corrupting influences and corrupt people within. Paul doesn't want Timothy to be surprised at the fact there are bad individuals within the church. Satan always sows weeds in the field where God has planted wheat (Matthew 13:24-30). The net of the gospel always pulls in both good and bad fish (Matthew 13:47-52). As Matthew Henry

---

[17] This wasn't the continent of Asia but the Roman province, the western most province of Asia Minor, modern-day Turkey.

says, 'Two traitors within the garrison may do more hurt to it than two thousand besiegers without.' However, one reason that Jesus told us to be careful not to concentrate on trying to remove the weeds is that good people can sometimes surprise us with a bad trait or bad behaviour that disappoints, and bad people are occasionally capable of extraordinary kindness or good behaviour.

We are not very good at distinguishing the weeds from the wheat. We cannot see the heart of a person and the motives behind their actions, but God looks at the source of their words and actions. Jesus spoke of wolves in sheep's clothing, of how a person can appear to be one thing when they are something completely different (Matthew 7:15). Such a wolf may look like a sheep, walk like a sheep, 'baa' like a sheep, smell like a sheep and be a very convincing imitation of a sheep. But as convincing as they may be, they will still possess the heart of a wolf and in certain circumstances will lose their sheep-likeness and reveal their true character.

In his second letter to young Timothy, the last letter Paul wrote, we have a picture of a lonely man, bereft of friends and helpers, in need of his scrolls (4:13), seemingly without even a coat for the coming winter (4:13, 21), and longing for the company and encouragement that Timothy would bring, 'Do your best to come to me quickly' (4:9), 'Do your best to get here before winter' (4:21). Yet, for all his disappointments and discouragements and his uncertainty about the future, one cannot read that letter without a sense that Paul would not have it any other way. He has found all that he wants in Jesus. He knew how previously in his hour of need, when deserted and alone, the Lord had stood with him and given him strength, and that gave him confidence and faith that the Lord himself would take care of him and bring him safely into his heavenly kingdom through whatever lay ahead (4:16-18).

There are three particularly remarkable things about this letter: Paul's lack of any self-pity despite his deplorable situation, the joy and certainty that pervades the letter and Paul's overwhelming con-

154

cern for his young leader, Timothy.

It's as if Paul is saying to Timothy, "I tell you all this, not to gain your sympathy and pity ... but rather for your sake, so that when such things happen to you, you will realise what is going on and know that you are not the first to experience such things." He went on to say, 'In fact, everyone who wants to live a godly life in Christ Jesus will be persecuted, while evil men and imposters will go from bad to worse, deceiving and being deceived' (3:12-13).

Although Paul prayed fervently that some of the things that he had to endure might be taken away (2 Corinthians 12:8), as Jesus did in Gethsemane (Matthew 26:39), he knew God well enough to accept that which God chose not to remove, in the knowledge that God's grace was sufficient to sustain him (2 Corinthians 12:9). 'That is why, for Christ's sake, I delight in weaknesses, in insults, in hardships, in persecutions, in difficulties. For when I am weak, then I am strong (v. 10). He treated both the bitter and the sweet experiences as though they were the same, as he did accolades and insults, praise and persecution, testifying to the truth that, 'I have learnt to be content whatever the circumstances. I know what it is to be in need, and I know what it is to have plenty. I have learned the secret of being content in any and every situation' (Philippians 4:11-12).

In 1 Corinthians 15:9 Paul says, 'For I am the least of the apostles and do not even deserve to be called an apostle,' and in Ephesians 3:8 he writes, 'Although I am less than the least of all God's people, this grace was given me: to preach to the Gentiles the unsearchable riches of Christ.' Paul's self-effacing, self-denying, low view of himself was undoubtedly a view shared by many of his enemies in the church. Many of them even questioned his right to be an apostle (1 Corinthians 9:1-2, 2 Corinthians 12:12). Many spoke ill of him, sought to damage his reputation and standing, and asserted themselves in preference to him.

It isn't easy to look back 2,000 years and discover exactly how things were on the ground at that time. For all we know, those 'super apostles' could have written more letters than Paul did, letters that have been lost to us. Maybe, at the time, any mention of Paul and what he was doing would have only been in small print on the back page of the Early Church Times, while others of whom we know nothing now, made the front page banner headlines! Despite statistical improbability, the truth may be that God mysteriously preserved those letters of Paul together with Luke's precious account of his travels and ministry. Perhaps God lifted these gold nuggets from a mountain of dross, sifted those grains of wheat lost in a mass of tares, only when Paul's life's work was completed. Could Paul ever have imagined how one day letters, written to specific individuals or churches, would be read in nearly every language under the sun by millions throughout the world?

Paul had but one desire, and he encouraged others to have it too, 'Do your best to win full approval in God's sight, as a worker who is not ashamed of his work, one who correctly teaches the message of God's truth' (2 Timothy 2:15 GNV). Such a person never promotes himself, never elevates himself or seeks the approval and praise of others. Paul willingly took the lowliest road of ignominy. 'For it seems to me that God has put us apostles on display at the *end* of the procession. We have been made a spectacle to the whole universe, to angels as well as to men. We are fools for Christ … To this very hour we go hungry and thirsty, we are in rags, we are brutally treated, we are homeless. We work hard with our hands. When we are cursed, we bless, when we are persecuted, we endure it, when we are slandered, we answer kindly. Up to this moment we have become the scum of the earth, the refuse of the world' (1 Corinthians 4:9-13).

As with Jesus, Paul lived what he taught. 'I die every day, I mean that brothers,' he wrote to the Corinthians in his first letter (15:31). Paul learned to make his body his slave (1 Corinthians 9:27), when for most people their bodies are their masters. It is so easy to be controlled by our desires and appetites, to become addicted to the things we like or fancy, whether or not they are sinful or harmful

156

things. Paul spoke of those whose 'god is their stomach' (Philippians 3:19).

I remember organising a twenty-four hour fast one Sunday at our corps. Those who could would stay and pray and share together over the lunch hour, (never the easiest time when fasting), following our morning worship. The elderly, those with children, those with health issues, diabetics and the like, plus anyone with other reasons for not joining in were encouraged not to feel bad about it. No one was to judge anyone else. Whilst shaking hands with one young man leaving the hall with his wife and two toddlers, he smiled and said, 'It's OK for you Captain, but I like my Sunday roast!' The inference was obviously that I didn't. He missed completely the purpose and point of it all.

Paul never forgot what he had been. He had been complicit in the persecution and murder of Christians. Yes, he knew that the Lord had forgiven him, even him, but he never forgot what he had done and/or who he had been prior to meeting Jesus. Neither did he try to keep his past hidden. No, for by his testifying to the truth about his past he brought hope to those who might otherwise think they were beyond God's grace. Obviously, there were those who looked down on him as a result of his honesty. Sadly, on that subject, things haven't changed. Even today there are those in the church who look down on others because of their background or past, even if they have undergone a complete transformation and are not the people they were.

Paul believed that in his Christian life there was never anything to be boastful about. We are saved through the grace of God alone, not by virtue of our abilities, sacrifice, achievements, or anything else we have (Ephesians 2:9). In 1 Corinthians 1:26-31, he reminds his readers of how God called them when many of them would have been classified as social failures, rejects. What had been achieved through such 'weak,' 'lowly,' and 'despised things,' had been achieved through Christ Jesus. Warning them of the dangers of boasting of what they had done, he commands them, 'Therefore, as it is written: "Let him who boasts boast in the Lord."'

There was only one time when Paul boasted about himself, and he did that very reluctantly. It was not to set himself upon a pedestal to be looked upon as superior to his fellows, but to counter the claims of 'false apostles, deceitful workmen, masquerading as apostles of Christ' (2 Corinthians 11:13). They were the men that he described as 'super apostles' (v. 5). Paul had humbled himself before the Corinthians, (v. 7), but unfortunately this had been misunderstood by those who were more impressed by the credentials that false prophets proudly boasted about and claimed were their qualifications for ministry. Whilst Paul, with love and respect, had elevated his listeners (v. 7) by denigrating himself, these charlatans had done the reverse. They had elevated themselves and exploited the people, taken advantage of them, and shown disregard and disrespect towards them.

One can imagine Paul's reluctance to boast. Speaking metaphorically, he was forced to go to a drawer that had been closed for many a long year and take out his dust-covered qualifications, feeling foolish at even the idea of displaying them publicly. He would much rather have kept them hidden from view, for to him they qualified him for nothing. But with the foolish judgement that the Corinthians had made when comparing him with his adversaries, it was a case of 'needs must.'

'Are they Hebrews? So am I. Are they Israelites? So am I. Are they Abraham's descendants? So am I. Are they servants of Christ?' Here he pauses and reiterates his discomfort of having to go down this route and speak as he is speaking. Having shown himself to be equal in pedigree to those false prophets, in answer to his final question he steps out further.

'I am more. I have worked much harder, been in prison more frequently, been flogged more severely, and been exposed to death again and again' (v. 22-23). He then goes on to list all the threats to his life he experienced during his ministry, before continuing to boast about his spiritual experiences in the following chapter. He ends it all by stating how he would prefer to boast about his weaknesses for it is in his weakness and dependency on God that God comes and equips him with power. 'That is why, for Christ's sake, I delight in weaknesses, in insults, in difficulties. For when I am weak, then I am strong' (12:10).

There is a secret, hidden path that few take. We prefer the mountaintop to the valley, strength rather than weakness, acclaim rather than insults, ease rather than difficulties. We avoid the route that would take us to where we might not see our way, where a way might seem impossible, even when Christ beckons and says 'take up your cross and follow me.' But those who step out in obedient faith discover God's special grace, sacred moments, closer company, and his hand upon them in a unique way.

'I have made a fool of myself,' Paul says in conclusion, 'but you drove me to it' (v. 11). He knows, as we all do, that however pure our motives might be, there will always be those who believe that what we do is from self-interest, even if we do 'die every day.' Paul was no fool, despite his claim to be one. People who live close to God are never fools except in the eyes of the world. Paul knew what might well be going on in the minds of his readers following his uncharacteristic boastful word, how some people might well think he said what he said because it mattered to him what others thought; that he was defending himself and his companions (v 19), but this was never the case. His concern was always what God made of what he said and did. The only reason Paul wrote what he did, (and that applied to the whole of his letter) was to strengthen his readers. He was forced to write what he did for their sake, to help his readers to see the wood for the trees as it were, and not to be deceived any more.

Paul, like Jesus, in a sense, died long before he met his death from the blade of the axeman in Rome[18]. No more clearly is this seen than his final words to the Ephesians on his journey to Jerusalem. 'And now, *compelled by the Spirit*, I am going to Jerusalem, not knowing what will happen to me there. I only know that in every city the Holy Spirit warns me that prison and hardship are facing me. However, I consider my life worth nothing to me, if only I may finish the race and complete the task the Lord Jesus has given me – the task of testifying to the gospel of God's grace' (Acts 20: 22-24).

---

[18] According to tradition St Paul was beheaded on the orders of Emperor Nero on the road to Rome's port of Ostia.

CHAPTER 18

OBSCURITY AND FAME

A survey taken in Britain among five to eleven year old children discovered that the top three things they wanted to be when they grew up were sports star, pop star and actor. Twenty-five years earlier the top three aspirations for that same age group were teacher, banker and doctor. In Britain, for a child to miss more than two days from school in any half-term to perform on stage or in film, requires a child performance licence from the local council. In five years, the issue of these licenses have increased by 80%. Stagecoach, the performing arts school franchise, reports that in the twelve years that followed 1999, student numbers increased from 12,000 to 36,000. In an American musical comedy show on television called 'Glee,' which was popular among teenagers, Rachel Berry, one of the characters in it, light-heartedly said, 'Nowadays being anonymous is worse than being poor.' Light-hearted it may have been, but for many people, young people in particular, there is an element of truth in what she said.

We live in a celebrity culture. There has been a proliferation of magazines such a 'OK' and 'Hello' full of glossy pictures revealing the lives of pop stars, sports stars and stars of stage and screen. The spread of the internet has resulted in fans following their stars' every move on Facebook, Twitter and the like. Most people want to be appreciated, valued and admired, and many believe the answer is found in fame and riches, to be like the celebrities they idolise. Some see the possibility of being discovered on a reality television talent show as being a fast track way to achieving what they desire. Is it little wonder that these shows are so popular?

But before we condemn the present generation we need to ask ourselves whether this desire is really something new? Why did young children a generation earlier aspire to be teachers, bankers and doctors? Surely such young children would have known little of what was really involved in such professions? What they might well have been aware of though, was that people in those professions were highly regarded and respected by adults. In other words their aspirations were the result of a desire to be 'something,' to be appreciated, valued and admired.

Whilst not everyone is part of our modern 'fame for fame's sake' culture, most people want to do something with their lives, to leave their mark, to achieve something, to do well, to get to the top of their chosen vocation. They certainly do not want to be disregarded, looked down on or considered a nonentity. As different as we all might be, the last thing any of us would want is to be forgotten, for our lives to have counted for nothing.

As Christ's life ebbed away, one of the scoundrels nailed to a cross alongside his cried out to him a simple request. He was a criminal, a thief. He recognised that he was being punished justly (Luke 23:41). He recognised too that Jesus was no criminal. More than that, he seemed to realise that hanging next to him was more than just an ordinary man, that Jesus had something, was someone unique, that he was a man without sin. He seemed to have grasped what his disciples failed to grasp despite all Christ's teaching and their time in Christ's company, that his kingdom was not of this world. Maybe, as he awaited his fate in a cell in Pontius Pilate's dungeon, he had heard what his fellow prisoner had dared to say when he faced Pilate (John 18:36). Now, as he watched Jesus close-up and saw how he accepted the injustice of his humiliation, shame and suffering, he caught a glimpse of the exceptional nature of the one who was hanging there beside him.

That cry from the thief's lips is essentially a prayer, a petition from a dying robber to a dying Saviour. It is full of humility. He confessed that he was guilty, that he was a sinner deserving of punishment. He knew that he did not deserve anything from this Jesus, but having caught a glimpse of who Jesus was and where he was going, he made the smallest of requests – that he, Jesus, might remember him.

Most of us will be forgotten in less than a hundred years. There will be few signs that we ever existed. Those who ever really knew us will be gone. There are those who gain fame, whether by accident or design, who will find their names and possibly stories recorded somewhere. Yet, can they and all that they have been, ever really be remembered? Can the truth of who any of us were, and what we did, and what we were truly like, ever be captured and known by future generations? Like so many of us, all that penitent thief wanted was for someone to remember him. That is all he asked. He perhaps hoped that from time to time in his eternal kingdom Christ's thoughts might return to these moments spent with this fellow sufferer.

Like the Syro-Phoenician woman of Mark 7:26, the penitent thief would have been grateful for mere crumbs from Christ, (v. 28). But Christ isn't in the business of dispensing crumbs. It is not in his nature. He wasn't prepared to give crumbs to the woman and he was not now prepared to give crumbs to this man. Neither of them was deserving of what he gave, but both received his grace and mercy in abundance. When God gives he always gives lavishly, abundantly.

'I tell you the truth,' said Jesus, (did he ever do otherwise?)

163

'... today,' yes, this very day, the worse day of your life, '...you will be with me in paradise.' In his commentary on this passage, William Barclay reminds us that Paradise 'is a Persian word meaning *a walled garden*. When a Persian king wished to do one of his subjects a very special honour he made him a companion of the garden which meant that he was chosen to walk in the garden with the king.' Can there be anything more wonderful than to be with Jesus in that heavenly garden? That man's worst ever day was to become a day more wonderful than any he had ever had, or that he could ever have imagined.

Contrast that man's humility and sense of undeservedness with the attitude we find in two incidents that took place earlier in the gospels, following Christ's Transfiguration. Jesus' attention was turning towards making that final journey with his disciples to Jerusalem. What took place on Mount Hermon was a turning point in his ministry. Jesus had already spelt out clearly what was awaiting him when he got to Jerusalem, and in response Peter had remonstrated with him before then being severely chastised by Jesus, (Mark 8:31-33). As the little band travelled back together through Galilee, a journey that would eventually take them to Jerusalem, Jesus again broached the subject with his disciples, again predicting what lay ahead of him (Mark 9:31). But the next verse tells us, 'they didn't understand what he meant and were afraid to ask him about it.'

When they arrived at Capernaum Jesus was aware that following this second disclosure the disciples had spent their time quarrelling as they walked along. So he asked them what the disagreement had been about, even though he knew exactly what they had been arguing about. No doubt embarrassed, they refused to tell him, (v. 33-34). God knows everything about us, all we think, say or do, but he does like to hear the facts from us. He likes us to acknowledge the truth. That is what confession is, acknowledging what God already knows.

They had been arguing about who was the greatest, or more accurately (as Luke 9:46 tells us), 'which of *them* would be the greatest.' The desire to be top dog, top of the pile, in charge, the greatest, is the cause of most of the problems in the world and, sadly, even in the church. How often has there been dissension in the local church over someone being given a role or a position that another thought they were more entitled to or qualified for? Whilst it is rare for someone to see another preferred and to bear no ill will or resentment towards them, it ought to be normal among Christians. As Paul implores us, '... in humility consider others better than yourself' (Philippians 2:3). Some Christians can appear saintly until tested in this way.

William Sangster[19] records a fable that Oscar Wilde used to tell. The Devil was once crossing the Libyan Desert when he came upon a group of small fiends who were tempting a holy hermit. They tried him with the seductions of the flesh; they sought to sow his mind with doubts and fears; they told him that all his austerities were worth nothing. But it was all to no avail. The holy man was impeccable. Then the Devil stepped forward. Addressing the imps he said, "Your methods are too crude. Permit me for one moment. This is what I would recommend." Going up to the hermit he said, "Have you heard the news? Your brother has been made Bishop of Alexandria." The fable says "A scowl of malignant jealousy clouded the serene face of the holy man."'

Jesus knew exactly what his disciples had been arguing about, and as a result we read, 'Sitting down, Jesus called the twelve'(Mark 9:35). When a rabbi sat down to speak to his disciples it meant that he had some pronouncement, something very important, something out of the ordinary, something very serious to say; something that his listeners really needed to take on board. 'If anyone wants to be first,' Jesus said, 'he must be the *very* last, and the servant of all'

Even as Jesus spoke he knew that his words would need clarifying. He understood how the human mind worked. He knew how people wanting to be 'something', wanting recognition, wanting to get on in the world, tend to target those who might help them

---

[19]   In both his book, 'He is Able' and also his 'Daily Readings' page 200

achieve their ambitions, people with influence, people with power. We have a saying in this country, 'It's not what you know but who you know.' Despite both the example of his life and all that Jesus taught, it happens in church and with church. A well-dressed stranger who appears to be a professional man can find himself welcomed with open arms, especially if he has talents or other assets that the church desperately needs. Yet, is the welcome always as enthusiastic for someone who is obviously going to be a problem or require a disproportionate amount of our time and help? One individual is attractive, the other might well be repulsive, but how did and does Jesus value them both?

As institutions, churches of various persuasions have a poor record in this area. Often they have sought to curry favour with authority or potential benefactors to the neglect of fulfilling their God-given mission. Often the church's desire for greatness, for respect, acceptance, affection, influence, social standing, prestige, position, and an elevated place in the public mind have displaced its prime task which should also be its prime desire, to seek and to save the lost. Following a Saviour who was ostracised, stigmatised and crucified by the establishment is not easy. Churches have spent an inordinate amount of time, effort and money in their desire to remain inside the city walls of the establishment, sometimes even selling their very soul to do so.

In wishing to clarify, to make clear what he meant by his words, Jesus then took a child and had him stand in their midst (Mark 9:36). Now a child is not influential or powerful. A child cannot give us power, influence, promotion, position. A child cannot give us things. A child is always in need. We will always have to provide for a child, and our commitment to a child will also limit our own personal freedom. It is significant that Jesus does not leave the child to just stand among his disciple band. No! He then picks the child up and embraces him/her, adding, 'Whoever welcomes one of these little children in my name welcomes me, and whoever welcomes me does not welcome me but the one who sent me' (v. 37).

The story about the turning point in the life of St. Francis is a well known one. Francis had a natural horror of lepers according to Thomas of Celano. On his death-bed, St Francis himself stated, 'when I was in sin, it seemed too bitter for me to see lepers.' One day when riding his horse near Assisi he met one. 'He felt terrified and revolted.' He was torn between what he felt and what God would have him do, but 'he dismounted from his horse and ran and kissed him. As the leper stretched out his hand, expecting to receive something, he received not only the money he hoped for but a kiss, something he could never have anticipated. No-one ever kissed lepers. Francis immediately mounted his horse and, although the field was wide open without any obstructions, when he looked around he could not see the leper anywhere.'

Of all the things in the world, lepers were what Francis despised the most. It was the most natural and normal thing in the environment in which he lived to ignore and refuse to interact with lepers. Culturally, that was what all respectable people did. Yet, despite that cultural norm and despite his own personal aversion to having anything to do with them, Francis embraced one.

It is easy to embrace friends and family. It is easy to embrace pleasant, kind and clean people, ... attractive people. It costs us nothing and we might even benefit from so doing. But to embrace someone who we and the world find repugnant, unlovable? Someone who has no memory of ever being accepted, valued or loved? Jesus would have us welcome those the world looks down on, the little ones. A real welcome is more than handing out a hot drink, a food parcel, a set of clothes, though none of these are without merit. Jesus would have us do all of that. A real welcome is more than allowing them into our company. We can do that and still leave plenty of space between them and us. A true welcome would embrace that needy one in such a way as to make them sense the message, 'We love you and want you to be part of our family.' But is that true? Do we really want

167

the likes of them to be part of our family? Jesus did not leave that child standing there, he swept that little one off his/her feet before then embracing them. 'As you did it to one of the least of these my brethren you did it to me' (Matthew 25:40, AV).

But before we condemn those disciples too harshly for being preoccupied with themselves rather than Jesus, I wonder what our response would have been had we been part of that disciple band? Indeed what do *we* discuss as we stroll along behind him? Jesus said, 'Therefore I tell you, do not worry about your life, what you will eat or drink; or about your body, what you will wear' (Matthew 6:25). 'Yet are not these very things the very centre of much of our conversation?' says Halford Luccock. 'There are multitudes of people who hardly ever talk about anything but food and drink and clothes. We often have the feeling that some of them could write their whole autobiography on a menu card. The journey from appetizer to dessert is their spiritual odyssey.'

Jesus now moved things up a gear. Luke 9:51 tells us how he 'resolutely set out for Jerusalem,' and again, a third time Jesus tells his disciples what is to happen to him when they get there (Mark 10:32-34). The response of James and John is incredulous (v. 35-40). They go to him, obviously out of earshot of the others, (v 41), and ask, 'Teacher, we want you to do whatever we ask.' Sometimes *our* prayers are like that. We expect Jesus to do whatever we ask. We have read of him saying, 'I will do whatever you ask in my name' (John 14:13), without realising the significance of the proviso, 'in my name.' What we ask for must be in accordance with God's will, for Christ's sake, to advance his cause, to enhance God's glory. Sometimes we may think our prayers fit that requirement when the truth is that our requests are merely what we *imagine* is best for God's cause. No wonder that even St Paul himself admits, 'We do not know what we ought to pray for' (Romans 8:28). The key is to be filled with his Spirit so that his Spirit expresses through us what might never occur to us, what we are incapable of expressing ourselves, and what is in absolute harmony with our Father's will. James and John had a lot to learn.

'Let one of us sit at your right and the other at your left in your glory,' they requested (Mark 10:37). They certainly had a very high view of their own importance and worthiness in seeking such prominence. Again, despite what Jesus had so recently said, i.e. 'If anyone wants to be first, he must be the *very* last, and the servant of all' (Mark 9:35), somehow the message had not got through to them. It's as if they had never heard it. Sadly, they make no reference to what should have been the distressing news that Jesus had just shared with them ... for the third time! There are no questions about it, no distress about it, no concern whatsoever for the One they claim to love and what lies in store for him. And when the other disciples heard what those two brothers had requested, they were no better. Yes, they may not have made such an egotistical request, but their indignation at what James and John had requested revealed that they were just as self-concerned. Whilst they may not have made the request, they would have been upset had John and James been given what they asked for.

We are immersed in a competitive culture, and however we might like to disguise the fact, it seeps into our individual souls as well as into our churches. We are a profit-driven society. We are daily bombarded by the media in one form or another with themes that arouse every unholy emotion in us: envy, covetousness, pride, vanity, greed. We live in a society where the desire for pre-eminence is seen as normal and acceptable and something to be sought. Rags to riches stories are admired as something to be emulated, whilst riches to rags by choice is definitely considered as something abnormal, and those who venture in a direction other than that considered 'normal' are thought of as strange indeed.

Charles Thomas Studd, (known as CT Studd) was one of three famous cricketing brothers. They were at Eton together in 1877 when their father got converted. He arranged to meet them in town and take the three of them out. They thought they would be going to the theatre or the Christy Minstrels. Imagine their shock when they discovered it was a 'God Talk' by the great American evangelist Dwight Moody. 'Before that time I used to think religion was a Sunday thing, like one's Sunday clothes, to be put away Monday morning,' Charles later said. 'We boys were brought up to go to church regularly but, although we had a kind of religion, it didn't amount to much. It was just like having a toothache. We were always sorry to have Sunday come, and glad when it was Monday morning. Then all at once I had the good fortune to meet a real live play-the-game Christian. It was my own father.'

His father wanted so much for his sons to know Jesus, but until they too got saved they were none too pleased with the change in him. However, when the three boys were home during the school holidays, a friend of their father who was staying with them managed to get each one on their own, unbeknown to the others, and during the course of conversation led them each to Christ.

All three brothers played cricket for Eton XI and then went on to play for Cambridge University, on one occasion beating the touring Australians by six wickets, a match that made CT's name. He and one of his brothers, George, (GB), went on to play for England. Both took part in the famous test match when Australia beat England for the first time ever and the term Ashes came into existence, following a humorous epitaph to English cricket published in the Sporting Times. Of the three, only Kynaston, (known as JEK), witnessed for Jesus to his team mates. In fact CT became a backslider for six years. Only cricket mattered to him. He later testified at how, during that period, he lost the joy he had when first he found the Lord.

It was when his other brother George was thought to be dying, and he watched him hovering between life and death, that he started to think of what use to George was all the popularity in the world now. 'What is all the fame and flattery worth? What is it worth to possess all the riches in the world, when a man comes to face eternity?' The words, 'Vanity of vanities, all is vanity' (Ecclesiastes 1:2

AV), kept echoing in his mind.

The experience changed Charles and resulted in him recommitting himself fully to God. 'CT was not a "born cricketer," nor was cricket to him just a pastime to wile away spare hours. He made a serious business of it,' says Norman Grubb, his biographer, 'and he set himself to get to the top of the tree at cricket.' Whilst he never regretted playing cricket and he was able to apply much that he learnt from it to other areas of his life, he regretted the fact that it became an idol to him: 'I realised my life was to be one of simple, childlike faith, and that my part was to trust, not to do. I was to trust in him [God] and he would work in me to do his pleasure.'

It wasn't long before he sensed God calling him to leave his privileged life and all the fame that he had and go to China. He faced opposition to his decision from the family, expressed especially in the tears of his broken-hearted mother. There were also godly people that Charles regarded highly who thought he was making a big mistake and tried to dissuade him. But, convinced of God's calling on his life, he willingly went and buried himself in the interior of China. In addition to leaving fame for obscurity, when CT Studd inherited a fortune from his father on his twenty-fifth birthday, he took Christ's words, 'Sell all ye have and give alms' (Luke12:33, AV), and 'Lay not up for yourselves treasures upon earth' (Matthew 6:19, AV), quite literally, and gave the whole of his fortune away.

These are the words he wrote to his mother in one of his letters, 'Oh! How I wish I had devoted my early life, my whole life, to God and his Word. How much I have lost by those years of self-pleasing and running after this world's honours and pleasures. What a simple life the Spirit lives out in us when he possesses us. It is so simple too, just to remember, 'I *have been* crucified with Christ,' I am dead. 'It is no longer I that live, but Christ that liveth in me.' My part is just to *let* him live in me.'

CHAPTER 19

HIS PLEASURE

When the Olympic Games came to London in 2012, the official theme music played during the Olympic Flame Relay, the opening ceremony, and every medal awards ceremony during the two weeks of competition was from the 1981 film, 'Chariots of Fire.' The film, which was set in the preparation for the 1924 Olympic Games in Paris, told the stories of Eric Liddell's athletic career and Christian faith, together with the story of his fellow athlete, Harold Abrahams (who was Jewish), and Abraham's fight against prejudice.

One of the most memorable quotations in the film is that of Eric Liddell, 'I believe that God made me for a purpose. But he also made me fast, and when I run I feel his pleasure.' Sadly, it is wrongly attributed to Eric. It was in fact a line created by the film's writer, Colin Welland. Having said that, it did reflect what drove Eric to win. Both a formidable rugby player, (he played six matches for Scotland), and a successful sprinter, he was already well known before he decided to concentrate on his athletics. When Liddell was invited to become an evangelistic speaker, he saw how his success in sport might provide an ideal platform to reach those who might otherwise show no interest in the gospel.

His purpose in running wasn't for personal fame and glory, but to bring glory to God, attention to his Saviour. He had already decided to return to China (the land of his birth), as a missionary long before the drama that would unfold at the Olympics. Three months prior to the British teams' arrival in France, Eric discovered the heats for the 100 metres, (his best prospect for winning a gold medal), were scheduled to be run on a Sunday. Because of his strong conviction that it was 'the Lord's Day' and that it was wrong for him to run, he felt obliged to inform the British Olympic Association that he could not take part. When his decision became public knowledge there was a hostile reaction to him. There were those who called him a traitor to his country. There were even some members of parliament who lambasted him for putting selfish beliefs before duty to country, but undaunted, he stuck by what he believed.

When he got to Paris, he was to be found preaching in the Scots Church in Rue Bayard on the Sunday in question, while Harold Abrahams prepared himself to win the 100 metres gold medal. His decision to remain true to his convictions and his God set him apart in the history of athletics. Although he loved running, and won the bronze medal in the 200 metres and then the gold in the 400 metres, a spectacular achievement indeed, he never allowed his sport to become the idol that, as we said in the previous chapter, cricket became to CT Studd. As The Guardian newspaper observed, 'Liddell has already decided that the race he has chiefly to run in the world is not on the cinder track.'

Our only purpose in all that we do and how we do it is to bring glory to God. We are set apart. Whilst others work for wages, we labour for our Master. Yes, we need money to feed the family, to pay the mortgage or rent, to clothe ourselves, but that is not the reason we do what we do. We do not go to work merely to please our employer or, as is the case in much of life today, to do the minimum work for maximum return. Our desire at the end of the day is to have

174

pleased the One who has done so much for us. We are first and foremost his servants. Whereas our culture today wants to get all it can *from* life, our desire is to give all we can *to* life.

'Therefore, I urge you, in view of God's mercy, to offer your bodies as living sacrifices, holy and pleasing to God – this is your spiritual act of worship' (Romans 12:1).

I was preaching on this text one Sunday morning and trying to explain that everything we do we do for Jesus. We should treat everything we do as though he was the recipient. Everything is an offering to him, an expression of gratitude to him for his abundant mercy, a response to his goodness to us. I went on to say that whether anyone notices – or not, appreciates what we have done – or not, thanks us – or not, gives us the credit for it – or not, will not matter, because the One we did it all for was Jesus. Our only concern ought to be whether we please him.

At the end of the meeting, as the congregation left and my wife and I shook their hands at the door, I noticed Dot, a little lady in her seventies who had recently been widowed, was standing against the wall opposite me, out of the queue. Whilst concentrating on each of the people as they came up and shook my hand I watched her hovering there and guessed that, being shy, she was waiting until the queue abated before approaching me.

She was a lovely lady, a simple soul who had had a very hard life. Often, when I visited her she would apologise for the fact that she didn't think she was very bright. But I could see something really special in her. I thought of the words, 'But God chose the foolish things of the world to shame the wise; God chose the weak things of the world to shame the strong. He chose the lowly things of this world and the despised things – and the things that are not – to nullify the things that are, so that no-one can boast before him' (1 Corinthians 1:27-29).

'So when I am doing the washing up for the over 60s club,' she said, having stepped forward during a lull in the procession of

175

people leaving the hall, 'I'm not doing it for them?'

'No,' I replied.

'And I'm not doing it for you?' she continued, with a twinkle in her eye.

'No,' I again replied.

'I'm just doing it for Jesus?'

'Yes,' I answered.

'It was my idea to volunteer to do the washing up for the over 60s club,' she then stated, 'but you asked me if I could help with the washing up for the Alpha Course you are running didn't you? Even though you asked me, I'm still not doing it for you am I? It's all for Jesus.'

I looked down on this tiny woman and could have cuddled her had it not been that doing so in public might have embarrassed her. I thought to myself, 'There will be others, far more intelligent than she, who will not have thought any more about the message, never mind apply it to themselves.'

'I praise you, Father, Lord of heaven and earth,' said Jesus, 'because you have hidden these things from the wise and learned, and revealed them to little children. Yes, Father, for this was your good pleasure' (Matthew 11:25)

Dot enjoyed the company of the other ladies in the kitchen and they loved her. The plates and dishes were sometimes piled quite high, but she would quietly get on with the job with never a moan or grumble of any kind. But following our brief conversation that Sunday morning I noticed a difference in her countenance whenever I saw her at work in the kitchen, an added sparkle I had never seen before.

Making everything in our lives pleasing to God, God glorifying wherever we are, whatever we are doing, is what real worship is. If that is not what we are about during the week, then what we do in our Sunday 'worship' meetings is all empty noise and lacking integrity. Where is the consistency if what the Lord has seen all week isn't in

176

tune with what he observes on a Sunday? Surely, he will wonder about the love we claim we have for him? As he hears us singing songs about his Lordship, I wonder if our words grieve him? The fact is, that when Jesus is ever on our mind and we are continually seeking to please him in what we are doing, even the most menial, dirty, unpleasant, or boring task will be transformed.

I read of a Christian who worked in a factory but was unfulfilled in what was a monotonous and unpleasant job. He was quite miserable. It was an effort for him to motivate himself to get out of bed in the morning and go to work, such was the effect it had on him. So he decided to leave and find another job. But, wanting to ensure that he find the right job, the job where God would have him be, he asked his minister and his church friends to pray that the right job would come along and he would recognise it. They were faithful in their prayers for him, but weeks turned to months with no sign of an answer to their petitions

Finally, somewhat confused, bewildered and depressed, the man made an appointment to see the minister. The minister gave the man his full attention and, having listened to everything he had to say, made a suggestion, 'Maybe God wants you in that factory and for you to continue doing what you are doing. Have you ever considered that?'

'How can that be? I am so miserable there. God doesn't want me to be unhappy does he? He wants me to feel fulfilled, surely?' replied the man.

'That is true, but maybe there is something else he wants. Maybe there is something other than the job that he wants changed,' the minister suggested.

'What do you mean?'

'Well, first answer me a question. Are there many Christians in your workplace?'

'No, I'm one of the only ones.'

'Then God definitely needs that light that you possess to

177

shine in the darkness you have told me exists there.'

'To test out whether the Lord wants you there, I suggest that you make your sole reason for being there and your sole reason for doing what you are doing – Jesus! Work for him. Do whatever you do, not for your factory boss, not even for your own satisfaction, but for Jesus, as though he had requested it. Then come back to me in a couple of weeks time and let me know how you get on.'

Next time the man met the minister he was like a different man. Nothing had changed at the factory, the job was as monotonous and unpleasant as it ever had been, but the man's focus had changed. It wasn't about what he liked or how he felt any more, but whether his attitude, spirit, and quality of work was pleasing to Jesus. Those around him that were doing the same job and felt like he had done about it, saw the difference in him. Prior to his conversation with his minister, he had been a bit of a misery, a moaner at work. Now he radiated joy. The change in him caused those around him to ask questions and created opportunities for him to witness to his Saviour; something he hadn't done before.

I was walking in the countryside with two friends on one occasion when I had to bend down to retie one of my shoelaces. Whilst down on one knee I caught a glimpse of a tiny, spectacularly beautiful fungus, almost hidden in the grass. It was shaped like a parasol. About two centimetres in diameter, it had a small, light brown circle at the centre from which pale grey, tightly packed deep ribs or pleats ran out to the edge. I know nothing of fungi, but my well-informed friend told me it was a Parasola Plicatilis fungus. I remained crouched there for some time in wonder at my discovery. One would need to bend low to have been so blessed with such a moment. It turns out that this little chap is one of many short-lived grassland fungi that appear overnight following rain. The fruit-bodies develop, expand, shed their spores and decay within twenty-four hours, and by next morning there is little or no evidence that they ever existed.

The thing that struck me, and remains with me regarding that experience, is that that fungus was not concerned about where it found itself, nor yet whether anyone would ever see it and appreciate its beauty. Its business was not to question why it was where it was, but to do that for which it was created whilst it could. For all I know, we may have been the only people who ever saw its splendour. Then it occurred to me that all creation was praising God, worshipping God by simply doing what it was created to do, obeying the laws of physics, biology, chemistry and the like, laws that God himself put in place. In other words, obeying his commands.

> 'He sends his command to the earth; his word runs swiftly.
> He spreads the snow like wool and scatters frost like ashes.
> He hurls down hail like pebbles.
> Who can withstand his icy blast?
> He sends his word and melts them;
> he stirs up his breezes, and the waters flow.'
> Psalm 147: 15-18

Being what God created them to be and doing what he ordained them to do is surely what the psalmist, in Psalm 148, meant when he exhorted everything in creation to praise the Lord?

> 'Praise the Lord from the earth, you great sea creatures and all ocean depths,
> lightning and hail, snow and clouds, stormy winds that do his bidding,
> you mountains and all hills, fruit trees and all cedars, wild animals and
> all cattle, small creatures and flying birds.'
> Psalm 148:7-10

Francis of Assisi captured it in his wonderful hymn, 'All Creatures of our God and King,' with verses and lines like:

Thou rushing wind that art so strong,
Ye clouds that sail in heaven along
O praise him, alleluia!
Thou rising morn, in praise rejoice,
Ye lights of evening, find a voice:

O praise him, O praise him,
Alleluia, alleluia, alleluia!

Thou flowing water, pure and clear,
Make music for thy Lord to hear,
Alleluia, alleluia!
Thou fire so masterful and bright,
That givest man both warmth and light:

The flowers and fruits that in thee grow,
Let them his glory also show.

Let all things their creator bless,
And worship him in humbleness.

Have you ever taken a walk in the countryside, and as you looked at all the beauty and listened to all the sounds, have not felt as though the whole of creation is praising him? But the fact is that nothing in creation can do otherwise. Nothing that God created can be or do other than what he designed them to be or do, from the smallest particle within an atom to the largest mountains and volcanoes, or planets beyond the furthest reaches of the universe. When it comes to the proliferation of plant and animal life and the incredible, incalculable variety of species that exist, they all operate according to how they were designed by the One who created them, however their creation came about. Even any genetic changes through the years have been possible because of the inbuilt possibility that he put in place. The instincts and behaviour of animals are inbuilt, passed down generations through their genes. They have no choice but to be as they are. Their obedience and thus their worship of their creator is an involuntary thing. They can do no other than praise him.

Having said all that, he did create one creature with choice and that was we humans. We have a choice. We can live in intimacy with and obedience to him; such a life glorifies him and brings him pleasure. Or we can plot a course of our own choosing, which obviously grieves him. Christ's life of intimacy and obedience both glorified and pleased his Father.

'This is my Son, whom I love; with him I am well pleased' (Matthew 3:17)

In his obedience to his Father, even to death on a cross (Philippians 2:8), Jesus brought glory to his Father (John 12:28).

Some think that if only their circumstances were different, if only they had someone else's talents, abilities, or position, they could achieve great things for God. Yet God would have them seek how they can live to please him where they are. As a consequence, they fail to know that peace of heart that God desires for them, a peace they can know in even the worst of circumstances. In their concern over what they could do for him, given a different situation, they fail to discover what he is waiting to do *through* them in their present situation.

God will indeed propel some people into the spotlight or public eye and use them there. Pray for such people, as they are in a greater danger than the rest of us. If Satan can bring down someone who is high-profile, he can do far more damage to God's work than he could by destroying someone who is unknown. More damage is done by felling a mighty cedar than by destroying a Parasola Plicatilis Fungus.

Another danger in hankering after greater things is that we can fool ourselves into thinking it is all for God's glory when it is purely to make ourselves feel better, to have the acknowledgement and recognition that other Christians have. God isn't so interested in what we can do on a platform at a particular time, but what goes on in our hearts and how we are when out of the spotlight, when no one sees us, when there is no-one around. He is interested in what we do in secret, the things that no-one else knows about (Matthew 6:4, 6, 18).

Richard Wurmbrand, who was imprisoned for many years and frequently tortured on account of his faith, wrote of the joy of a life totally focused on Christ, 'Alone in my cell, cold, hungry and in rags, I danced with joy every night …sometimes I was so filled with joy that I felt I would burst if I did not give it expression.' Had he not survived we would never have known of his worshipping God in secret.

Those of you who feel as though your light is hidden, may one day be surprised at what God did through your faithfulness. Offer God the treasure of your heart. Some lost soul may one day stumble across you, like I stumbled across that fungus in the woods, and be transformed by what they discover. If it had a brain, that fungus could have questioned its usefulness, wondered what the point was and given up. When the Lord said, 'I know the plans I have for you' (Jeremiah 29:11), he never said that we would know what they were or what he was about. Don't withdraw your offering, don't give up. One day he will show you the wonderful things that he was doing that you knew nothing about.

During World War I, a man who had been shot lay dying in the trenches. A friend leaned across to him and asked if there was anything he could do.

He replied, 'No, I am dying.'

'Is there anyone I can send a message to for you?' his friend then asked.

'Yes, you can send a message to this man at this address. Tell him that in my last minutes what he taught me as a child is helping me to die.' The man was his old Sunday School teacher.

When eventually the friend got back to England and found him and gave him the message, the old man said, 'God forgive me. I gave up Sunday School teaching years ago because I thought I was getting nowhere. I thought it was of no use.'

When the widow woman came to where the offerings were put into the temple treasury, and then put in her 'two very small copper coins worth only a fraction of a penny' (Mark 12:42), she could have never guessed how God was going to exalt her humble offering and tell the whole wide world about her. As for those rich and, no doubt, influential people who 'threw' in large amounts, we know nothing of them or their gifts. That which was undoubtedly done quietly and privately, God has made known to billions of people and in doing so he honoured and still honours the woman who honoured him (1 Samuel 2:30).

CHAPTER 20

VACATING THE THRONE

'The Father loves me because I am willing to give up my life ...'
said Jesus.
John 10:17 GNV

When King Saul fell from God's favour and God rejected him as king, (1 Samuel 15:26), the thing he found hardest to do was to relinquish his throne and bow his knee to the one that God had anointed to replace him. On disobeying God a second time, disobeying very specific commands, Saul was told by Samuel, 'The Lord has torn the kingdom from you today and has given it to one of your neighbours – to one better than you' (15:28). But Saul was unwilling to accept God's verdict on him, to take orders rather than give them, to place himself under the authority of another and not do his own will but that of another. So, although he was no longer king in God's eyes, he continued to act as though he was. He still sat on the throne and still maintained an appearance of kingship, but no longer did he have God's approval and authority.

Saul started well. When God chose him he was humble, and

185

he saw himself as unfit and unworthy to lead the nation as its king. Initially he had placed himself under the authority of God, and God blessed him with success. But as soon as he was confirmed as king, he became more independent and less obedient, revealing an unwillingness to accept that he was appointed king under God, not a king in his own right. Consequently, God was forced to reject him as king and he never achieved what God planned for him when he chose him.

There is a well known English saying not found in the Bible, 'Be careful what you pray for, because you might get it.' God did not want Israel to have a king in the first place, but the people persisted in asking for one. They were warned of the consequences, but they insisted in their plea. Sometimes, if we keep praying for something that God in his wisdom would rather we didn't have, he will actually give it to us. Sometimes it is the only way he can teach us how foolish we are and how wise he is.

In Numbers 11, the Israelites moaned about their hardships. Their moaning angered God, and he then sent terrifying fire that burned some of the outskirts of the camp (v. 1). In response to the people's fearful cries, Moses prayed to God and the fire died down. What relief there must have been among the people. But they didn't learn their lesson, for we read that almost immediately the people started moaning again, this time about their monotonous diet, the food that God provided.

With all that God had done for them, they still felt that they had been better fed and better off in Egypt. 'If only we had meat to eat!' they wailed (v. 4-5). Their continual complaining so wore Moses down that he wished himself dead (v. 10-15).

In response, God was angry with the people and, as we read the verses that follow, we can almost hear him saying, 'You want meat do you? You are really insistent on having meat? All right I'll give you meat!' Moses told the people, '... The Lord heard you when you wailed, "If only we had meat to eat! We were better off in

Egypt!" Now the Lord will give you meat, and you will eat it. You will not eat it just for one day, or two days, or five, ten or twenty days, but for a whole month – until it comes out of your nostrils and you loathe it' (v. 18-20).

God wanted Israel to be a nation set apart, different from the other nations around it. He did not want them to have a king like other nations, for he, Jehovah God, was their king. But they wanted a king like other nations because they wanted to be like other nations (v. 20), 'with a king to lead us and to go out before us and fight our battles,' they said.

Tragically, the roles they described were all the roles of God himself. They are the roles that he desires to fulfill in our lives today if only we would let him. God wishes to lead us, go before us and fight our battles. But in their desire to be just like any other nation, the Israelites showed how they did not trust God, and how they didn't believe that his way was the best way. So often Christians desire to be like other people, to have what they have, live as they live. How often do we share the same aspirations and ambitions and make enjoying our lives our priority rather than seeking God's pleasure? We then wonder why we experience such discontent. It's hardly surprising that God seems so remote.

So it was that God told Samuel to give them a king in accordance with their wishes. Samuel complied with God's command and anointed the king God chose, a man who was very much the sort of king the people were wanting. He was taller than anyone else in the nation, an impressive young man without equal (9:2), truly a man's man. As Samuel stated to the people, 'Do you see the man the Lord has chosen? There is no-one like him among all the people' (10:24). Having previously shared God's unhappiness with what the people longed for, Samuel now seemed jubilant at God's choice of Saul as the people cried out, 'Long live the king!' But any joy that Samuel had was to be short-lived.

At his anointing, Samuel told Saul to go to Gilgal and await further instructions before striking the first blow against the Philistines. In fact, he was told to wait seven days. Saul did go to Gilgal and he did wait seven days, but it appears that he did not wait the whole of the seventh day. Sometime during that day, with the gathering storm of the Philistines massing and his own men deserting, plus the absence of Samuel, he became so anxious about his situation that he took matters into his own hands and offered burnt offerings to God. 'I felt compelled' (13:12), he was later to say when Samuel reprimanded him.

It was indeed a dire situation; all the more reason for him to wait on God. His partial obedience was not acceptable. Partial obedience is never obedience. Partial obedience is disobedience. What Saul did was religious in nature. We too might fulfil religious requirements and duties, even to the admiration of those around us, but religious activity is no substitute for obedience. Saul's response to Samuel's reprimand showed an independent spirit, something much admired in society today, but sadly something that all too often creeps into the church. God requires both our obedience to and dependence on him.

That one action revealed Saul's heart. He did not truly trust God and he failed to keep the terms of his appointment as king. He did not see himself as subservient to God's sovereignty, but as a king in his own right. 'You acted foolishly,' God told him through his prophet Samuel, '… your kingdom will not endure'(v. 13-14). That may seem rather severe. We may wonder whether we too would have seen no alternative had we been in the same dreadful situation that Saul was in. That is because we are all Sauls! Lots of us rarely see the wonder of what God himself can and will do because we are not prepared to wait on him/for him. Frequently God will test our love and faith by leaving it until the eleventh hour before he acts. It's scary. But how wonderful it is when God himself grabs success out of the jaws of failure.

Saul was then clearly commanded to destroy the wicked Amalekites, to totally annihilate both them and their animals (15:3). Now

Saul wasn't without virtue. Before he attacked the Amalekites, he allowed the Kenites nearby to get out of the way. But again, Saul only partially fulfilled God's command, he partially obeyed God, and as we have already said, partial obedience is actually disobedience. As with Adam so with Saul, disobedience was their great sin. When Samuel met up with Saul and challenged him, the prophet recalled how once Saul had been so small in his own estimation of himself (v. 17). It was God who chose him and God who elevated him through no merit of his own. But the humble man had become proud of himself, so much so that as Samuel discovered, Saul had even built a monument in honour of himself on Mount Carmel following the conflict (v. 12).

Again, Saul thought his religious observances and his sacrifice of the best of the Amalekites' animals to God would justify what he had done. He even claimed, and possibly thought, that he had obeyed the Lord (v. 20). This offence was more serious than the first as the command on this occasion was far more clearly God's express orders. Saul's offence confirmed just how disobedient and rebellious Saul had become. God's verdict this time was immediate. As far as God was concerned, Saul was no longer king. Samuel told Saul, 'The Lord has torn the kingdom from you today and has given it to one of your neighbours – to one better than you' (15:28).

Because he rejected the authority of God, Saul lost the authority God had previously given him. Though Saul admits he has sinned, there is no real conviction, humility, remorse, repentance. We too might not be in a position to deny what we have done when we have been caught out and the evidence against us is overwhelming. In such circumstances any expression of regret might be more to do with our concern for ourselves rather than genuine sorrow for sin. This seems to have been Saul's situation. He was concerned to save face in front of the nation's elders. He did not want them to know God's condemnation of him and to have Samuel disassociate himself from him (v. 30). He even went to worship! (v. 31). What does God make of the worship of those who are not totally surrendered to him?

I may as well kneel down
And worship Gods of stone,
As offer to the living God
A prayer of words alone

For words without the heart
The Lord will never hear;
Nor will he to those lips attend
Whose prayers are not sincere.
John Burton

God wanted everything of the Amalekites utterly destroyed and Saul failed to do as God wanted. There are things that God wants utterly destroyed in our lives, in us; things that we think not too bad, things that perhaps we think can be used for his service. This partial obedience is typical of the Saul in us. Like Saul, because we have messed up on so many occasions God has declared us flops and failures, unfit to rule the territory he gave us. That territory might be the responsibility we have at our workplace, in our home, in our church, or even that territory within us. As with Saul, he has torn that territory from us and given it to a neighbour – to one better than us. That neighbour that God has appointed, the Lord Jesus Christ, did not come to make us better Sauls, but to supplant us and take over from us. But, like Saul, we are not very good at letting go of the throne.

Jesus came to save us and to forgive us, but what real use are we to God if self is still king in his own right? If we still occupy the throne? The mess such a king made of it will be repeated again and again if he is left in that position, though it might appear otherwise.

Samuel was disappointed with Saul just as we might be disappointed with ourselves, with our failures. He mourned Saul's failure

190

in the same way as we might be upset with ours. The old king had failed. God had rejected him even though he was not prepared to accept God's verdict and abdicate. Consequently, he was never to fulfill what God had planned for him at the very beginning. God had said, 'He will deliver my people from the hand of the Philistines.' Despite his best efforts and some victories, he would never free Israel from their enemy. In fact, eventually he would die fighting them (I Samuel 31). Saul was a failure. All we Sauls are failures. Self improvement won't work. Herculean efforts to do better and to be better will fall short. God's answer was that Saul be replaced.

Samuel mourned over Saul's failure, but God wanted him to move on and leave the past behind. So, under God's guidance, Samuel went looking for the answer, the replacement of King Saul, among Jesse's sons. So too with us. Like William Booth, we might mourn over our failures:

My tempers are fitful, my passions are strong,
They bind my poor soul and they force me to wrong.

Now tossed with temptation, then haunted with fears,
My life has been joyless and useless for years.

Yet God would have us move on and realise that he has an answer to our sorry condition.

Eliab, the first of Jesse's sons that Samuel saw, looked every part a king ... just like Saul had done. But the Lord had to tell Samuel not to consider appearance or height. This king would be different. 'The Lord does not look at the things man looks at. Man looks at the outward appearance, but God looks at the heart' (16:7). One by one Samuel examined every son presented to him and God's response was negative to all seven of them.

One could look on each of these sons as representing the various things that Christians look to in search of the victorious life that

191

eludes them. These include tasks we must do, goals we must achieve, rules we must keep, people we must copy, spiritual experiences we must have. There are many more man-made things that people think will be the answer to what they lack. But they all involve striving, strain and stress. They all involve our efforts. Consequently, if we achieve any success it results in pride, and if we don't, the result is despair.

So it was that Samuel asked Jesse if he had any more sons. There was one, but even his father Jesse didn't consider him a possible candidate. He had left him out tending the sheep when he called all his sons together. But the moment Samuel set eyes on young David, God told him, 'Rise and anoint him; he is the one' (16:12).

God had not rejected Saul as a person, only as king. There is now to be another king, Saul's replacement. David is anointed, but no-one seems to know and David does nothing to gain recognition for himself. He patiently waited in the wings until the time came when he took on the challenge of Goliath (I Samuel 17). Saul was the most formidable man the Israelites had and the biggest, but he was powerless against such a foe. Nowhere is Saul's failure and David's superiority more clearly seen. In this story we see something of Christ's victory on our behalf. Jesus triumphed where man could only fail.

Israel lacked a champion. 'Give me a man and let us fight together,' Goliath cried(17:10). Goliath dominated the Israelites. He was sure to defeat any man who tried to stand up against him, even Saul who was the best Israelite qualified for the task. However big, tall, powerful and capable we may appear, we are no match for Satan. 1 John 5:18 tells us, 'the whole world is under the control of the evil one,' who Jesus referred to as 'the prince of this world' (John 12:31).

Despite Saul's failure, God still loved him and wanted to save him. Goliath dwarfed David as Satan and his power dwarfs you and me, but we are simply told that God was with David. God provided his own champion to face Satan when Satan metaphorically cried,

'Give me a man.' Until Jesus came, Satan invariably defeated man. Like Jesus, David went alone to face his foe. Like Jesus, he went in weakness. Jesus had Peter re-sheath his sword and he did not call forth the legions of angels to save him as he could have done. He met might with weakness. 'The weakness of God is stronger than man's strength' (1 Corinthians 1:25). And as David's final blow against Goliath was with Goliath's own sword, so too did Jesus conquer Satan using the very weapon with which Satan sought to destroy him – death, his death on the cross.

One strange fact in this story is that although David was the harpist who brought such blessing and peace to Saul's troubled heart (I Samuel 16:14-23), when David was brought to Saul as he faced the Philistines, he did not recognise him. But then again, many are those whom Christ died to save, who do not recognise him to be the One who has been the source of every blessing they have. Though Saul was a failed and rejected king, God still loved him and had David save him. But God destined David not merely to be his saviour, but to be his king. God didn't save Saul for him to continue sitting on the throne. He saved him to supplant him, to take his place as the rightful king. Jesus did not come just to save us but to supplant us. Later on in the story we read how Saul invited David to sit at his table as a guest and how David could never sit at his table as a guest. Neither can Jesus remain just a guest, as though our heart and our home and our table all belong to us. He is the rightful king, the rightful owner of our heart, our home. He must be the host at the table. We are but honoured guests.

Though Saul would not accept David and in fact hated David, pursuing him with the intent of killing him, David never stopped loving Saul. He never gave up trying to win Saul. He never did anything to harm Saul, even when given two golden opportunities to get revenge in exchange for all the hate and venom that Saul had discharged towards him. He was all for Saul and wanted the best for him. That can be seen clearly by the way he wept bitterly when Saul died on the battlefield, (2 Samuel 1:12,17-27). At no time did David attempt to take the throne by force, even though he had the right to it. Neither will the Lord Jesus. He will only accept it by invitation, when we willingly vacate it.

But the story doesn't end there. In 2 Samuel 9, we see in David a further lovely illustration of Christ's love for fallen man when, now installed as King of Israel, he asks, 'Is there no-one still left in the house of Saul to whom I can show God's kindness?' or 'the kindness of God,' as the authorised version puts it, (v. 3). Normally a new king would annihilate all family members of the previous king, to ensure that there were no pretenders to his throne. In that culture it would have been considered quite normal and the right thing for a monarch to do. Saul's grandson Mephibosheth could have expected death when King David discovered he was alive and had him brought to his court, but David did what would have seemed absurd to any other country's monarch observing it. He invited him to eat at his table, not as some visiting guest, but permanently, as a son. In other words he adopted him.

Not only that, he restored to him all the land that had belonged to his grandfather. In what David did we see something of the magnanimity of God, the grace of God or, as David himself called it, 'the kindness of God.' We too are totally undeserving. Yet we, who were once his enemies, are invited to permanently sit at the table of which Christ is head, as his adopted children – thanks be to God through our Lord Jesus Christ.

CHAPTER 21

MY WAY

The stories of Saul and David provide detailed illustrations of the animosity between God and our sinful human nature. That nature desires to be in control, does not like to be told what to do, wants to be on the throne and will not relinquish it unless forced from it. One of the things by which the serpent tempted Eve, as she stood close to the tree whose fruit God had specifically said must not be eaten, was the suggestion that by eating of it she and Adam would become like God (Genesis 3:5). Something of that exists in all the temptations we have, even if we are unaware of it and would deny such a desire.

The nature we have, the nature we inherited, the nature we were born with, is abhorrent to God. It is rebellious. It wants to dominate, to be in charge of its own affairs, to be independent, to do whatever it wants whenever it wants. It will always want to have things done its own way. These characteristics are expressed in all sorts of ways in popular culture today. With, 'It's my life I can do what I want,' many people justify euthanasia, with 'It's my body,' many women justify abortion for purely social reasons.

A survey conducted by Co-operative Funeralcare revealed

that two thirds of the 30,000 funerals it conducted replaced hymns with pop songs and that for the seventh year running the most requested of these was, 'My Way,' by Frank Sinatra. Paul Anka, the writer of the song, said he was influenced to write the words having noticed the prevalence of 'me this' and 'me that' in the periodicals he was reading. The lyrics are words of pride and self-centredness to the point of arrogance. In a funeral setting they sound like a statement of defiance to God, emphasising the point that the deceased went right through life without needing, surrendering or acknowledging him. It sounds as if the deceased, where *they* requested that the song be played, is having a final 'cock a snook' at God, even if that is not the intention. 'I did it my way.'

The final verse even denies God, stating that if a man is not self-sufficient he has nothing and is nothing, even pouring contempt on the value of prayer, inferring that someone who kneels before God is deluded and doesn't express their true feelings. The song ends with the singer bragging that nothing was ever able to bend him or break him, that he took the blows and lived his life his own way.

One could call it the Anthem of our Age, an expression of the me, me, me-centred-culture we live in. I find it quite distressing that someone should choose such a song at the very point in their journey when they are to meet and answer to their Maker. Having said that, how much of that attitude still remains in we who claim to belong to Jesus?

It is quite something to arrive at the conclusion that we are the worst of sinners and are worthy only of God's wrath. The offence that a man is to God is something that only God himself can reveal to the heart of a man. Only the Holy Spirit himself can bring a man into a conscious awareness of how God sees him, to that deep conviction of his sinfulness and his helplessness before God and yet of God loving him. Only at that point, as he throws himself upon God's mercy and truly repents, accepting that God sent his Son to pay the price for his wickedness by his death on the cross, can he know his sins washed away by the blood of Jesus. He can actually know God's forgiveness as a result of inviting Jesus into his life, into his heart as his friend and Saviour. Many of you have known that glorious experience.

The problem for many of us though, is that we don't allow the Lord to complete the job he started. We might compare our life to a car. Before we received Jesus as our Saviour, we drove where we thought best, often choosing a road that looked attractive and promising, only to eventually discover that it was taking us nowhere. What looked like a super highway when we set out on it, eventually became a narrow lane that petered out to a dirt track, then nothing. We found ourselves in a wilderness.

Now I am told, (by women!), that men are the worst for being lost and making out that they are not. The wife asks them if they know where they are and where they are going and the answer is that of course they do, as they carry on driving, just hoping for a sign or landmark that will put them on the right track. So too with life. A man may well have arrived in a wilderness, but he drives on regardless, despite not knowing where he is or what his eventual destination might be. He will keep going despite any damage he is doing to his car, hoping, just hoping that he will find some sign that will point him to the road that will lead him to the fulfillment of all his hopes and dreams.

Should a man at last realise his foolishness; the fact that he is incapable of getting it right, his need to be rescued and his need of a saviour, what a delight is his to discover that great Rescuer, Jesus! No longer will he be driving alone. He has someone to refer to, someone to navigate, someone to guide him, to help him. At first, all goes well. Life is so much better with Jesus besides him in the passenger seat. But as time goes on he discovers things are not all that they initially appeared to be. Jesus is in the car, yes. He regularly refers to him, particularly when he arrives at a difficult junction where there are conflicting signs and a number of different routes to choose from.

Yet, having Jesus beside him he still seems to get it wrong more times than he gets it right. He still feels uncertain as to whether he is on the right road. Sometimes, sad to say, he even blames the Lord for the situation he is in or for allowing him to make the wrong decision.

If you ask a group of men, 'Those of you who are bad drivers, please put your hands up,' rarely will even one hand go up. Whilst they will probably be unanimous in agreeing that there are a lot of bad drivers on the road, none will claim that they are one of them. The problem with all of us is our slowness in admitting that, when it comes to life, we are all bad drivers. Jesus didn't offer to enter our lives and transform things by merely being a passenger giving us advice. If we truly want Jesus to help and guide us then he needs to be in total control. We need to relinquish the steering wheel and driving seat and indeed our ownership of the car and be prepared to be the passenger and not the driver.

Changing the metaphor, I read a story of a man who, when passing a particular house, pointed it out to his friend and said, 'that's my house.' Later on another man walking passed the self-same house said to the lady accompanying him, 'that's my house.' Finally, a few days later, a third man arriving at the garden gate of the house pointed to it and made exactly the same claim to the man with him, 'that's my house.' The question that was then posed was this: how could each of these men claim, 'that's my house.' The answer is that the first person was the builder who made it, the second was the man who purchased it, and the third was the one who actually lived in it. Likening our lives to that house, the point was then made that Jesus has every right to call us his own. He made us, he purchased us, bought us with his blood that was shed at Calvary, and finally, he lives within us.

The first step we take towards acknowledging his ownership is when we seek his forgiveness and invite him into our hearts. No longer is he on the outside with us making the occasional reference to him, (if we believed he was somewhere out there in the first place).

Before ever we knew the Lord, some of us who believed in his existence would call out to him in emergencies. Once the crisis was behind us we would continue with our life much as before, whether or not we sensed that he had responded to our prayers.

What a delight and blessing was ours when we first opened the door of our hearts and received Jesus as our Saviour. What a welcome guest he was. But the tragedy for many Christians is that that is where we left it, or rather where we left him, in the hallway, just inside the front door. Whilst we may frequently pop out from the lounge or dining room to seek his advice or blessing, he is very much a guest in *our* house. Graciously and lovingly he often responds to our requests with various blessings and benefits, but in practice we are in charge still. We possess all the house keys and we control what rooms he has access to. He loves us and expresses his great love for us even though we break his heart, even though things are not as he had hoped, as he had planned. He knows that we still do not possess all he has in store for us, all he has planned to give us because we still have not placed ourselves in subservience to him, dependence on him, despite our desire to live to please him. It's as if the final penny has not dropped.

We think the Christian life is all about what we can do for God with his help and guidance. We think that the more we do, the harder we work, the more we will achieve for him and the more pleased he will be with us. Many of our prayers are voiced in those terms. We are blind to the fact that he wants and needs to take full control and direct and do things himself, and that in fact we are incapable of doing what only he can do, or being what only he can be. The Christian life is more about what he can do for us and through us, rather than what we do for him.

In 1867, Emma, the wife of the American evangelist Dwight L Moody, was suffering with progressively worsening asthma. Her doctor advised that sea-air might cure her condition. Dwight had been particularly busy during the previous twelve months and decided that he could make up for what he felt might have been his ne-glect, by taking her on a sea voyage. He thought that if they could make their destination England, he too might benefit; firstly, by at-tending the Metropolitan Tabernacle to hear Charles Haddon Spurgeon, the 'Prince of Preachers,' and secondly, by hopefully hav-ing a meeting with George Muller of Bristol.

When he arrived in Bristol, George Muller took him to Ash-ley Down which was at that time on the edge of the city. Here Dwight saw the three huge buildings that had been built and now housed over 1100 orphans plus a further two that were still in the process of being built. Dwight was impressed. In conversation with the old man he spoke of the similarities between his own huge build-ing project back in Chicago, a massive YMCA with an auditorium that would accommodate three thousand people, and what Muller was doing. He told of all his hard work gathering funds and pledges from wealthy donors around the city. Muller quietly and patiently lis-tened. When he had concluded, Dwight then asked Muller how he had managed to fund his massive project?

Muller replied, 'I prayed, Dwight. I prayed.'

'I know that,' Dwight answered, 'but ...'

'That's all. I prayed. No running to the offices to ask men to give. Excuse me, but this is the truth. I did not ask anybody. And God always supplied.' Muller then went on to explain to Dwight that the issue wasn't so much about how to build a building as about Dwight Moody himself. He continued, 'It is not so much what Dwight, one young man who is just thirty years old, can do for God. This is what I hear you talk about. How many businessmen you asked. How you run around. How you get pledges. It is more – *what God can do for and through Dwight Moody!*'

Having allowed the Lord into our lives everything must be surrendered to his will and purpose. He must be given access to every room in the house and allowed to rearrange everything the way that he wants it to be, whatever we might prefer. A few years ago, my wife and I were in the vicinity of where we once lived prior to entering training to become Salvation Army officers several decades earlier. We decided that we would like to take a look at the house that had once been our home, and so we drove to the village just outside Northampton. It was a beautiful house overlooking farmland to the rear. When we pulled up in front of it, imagine our surprise when we saw that the rockery that I had painstakingly built right along the length of the front garden had been removed.

Also, two friends and I had dug out a vast quantity of stone and rubble, (the remains of a demolished cottage that previously stood on the site of our home), that had been used to fill an old well we had discovered underneath the lawn in our front garden. When we commenced our labours it was quite an easy task, but as we worked our way deeper things became much more difficult. We needed to pump out all the water that would accumulate between the weekends before we could work on the project. It became a very slow and arduous task, but eventually we completed it and had a twenty-one foot deep well with thirteen feet of water in it.

I then built a small stone wall around the well-head with a metal protective cover and a roof over it, like one sees in pictures of English cottage gardens. When my father came to stay, he made a windlass to which he attached the original chain that we had found buried in the rubble. Consequently, we were able to hoist up buckets of water for the garden when rain was not forthcoming. The finished job was such a picturesque feature in the garden that even the local press sent a reporter to investigate what we had done. However, as we now looked across the garden we could see that the well had gone! A subsequent owner had decided to cut a drive right through the lawn, demolishing all traces of what we had done in restoring that beautiful centre-piece. There were some quite alarming changes to the front of the house that were not to our liking too!

We had anticipated some cosmetic changes. We knew the house would not be the same as when we left it. Everybody's tastes are different. But we were not prepared for such a wholesale root and branch transformation. We foolishly thought that anyone following us would so appreciate what we had done with regards to those particular features, that we could be sure they would still be there. How wrong can you be? We soon realised that returning had not been a wise thing to do. We were better off savouring the memories of the house as we had known it. Consequently, we left the village saddened and not a little angry, would you believe? Angry? How ridiculous! It was no longer our house. It belonged to someone else. They had a right to do whatever they wished with it. It was never going to be ours again.

So too with our lives when we give up ownership to Jesus and we allow him to go through each room throwing out clutter and rubbish, that which will not enhance his work, maybe stuff that is dear to us. 'Don't you know that you yourselves are God's temple?' (1 Corinthians 3:16). If Jesus needed to cleanse the temple in Jerusalem for it to be fit for purpose, then he will surely need to do far more than make cosmetic changes in us for us to be fit for purpose. The action he needs to take might well be as severe as that which he took in Jerusalem the day after that first Palm Sunday all those years ago (Mark 11: 15-17). We might be reluctant to allow him to enter every room or every corner of it for fear of what he might do.

But the truth is that we cannot partially hand over the ownership, make him a partial Lord. He either owns it all or he doesn't own it at all, or as the saying goes, 'If he is not Lord *of* all then he is not Lord *at* all.' Without this total surrender, it will never be a case of living *his way*. However things may appear, however pious I might seem, however religious or sincere I might be, however much I pray about what I do and seek his help in doing it, it will remain a case of, *'I did it my way.'*

CHAPTER 22

THE GREAT DECEIVER

It was George Muller who said, 'Ninety percent of knowing God's will is choosing to have no will of your own. There was a day when I died; died to George Muller, his opinions, preferences, tastes and will. Died to the world, its approval or censure; died to approval or blame even of my brethren or friends. And since then have studied only to show myself approved by God.'

Most of us arrive at that point very gradually. Self is peeled away very slowly, layer by layer, like skins from an onion. This is often because we cannot see ourselves as we are. We cannot disentangle ourselves from the mix of motives that we have. We sincerely believe that what we are doing is the right thing, that it will glorify God when there is so much of ourselves in it all. Satan is known as the Great Deceiver, and that he certainly is. His greatest ability in that role is to get us to deceive ourselves. What was it that Eve said when God challenged her after she had taken and eaten the fruit that God had forbidden? 'The serpent deceived me and I ate.' (Genesis 3:13). The truth is that Eve deceived herself when she decided that doing other than what God desired would be more beneficial to her, and that his warnings were not to be taken seriously.

Having committed our lives to God, Satan knows that he cannot tempt us like once he did, and that the paths he once so easily led us down are now closed. With our eyes fixed on Jesus and a refusal to look back, Satan finds that the temptations he regularly used in the past are no longer the effective tools they once were. But he has innumerable tools of every kind in his toolbox. Once we belong to Jesus, he adopts more subtle approaches.

Seeing our desire to please God and achieve his purposes, Satan presents alternative ways to us to achieve what we believe are God's goals. And because we have such a clear view of where we want to get to, we often press ahead, praying that God will give us all we need to get there. Often we are blind to the fact that what we thought were his goals are often nothing of the kind, or in those instances where the goal we are pursuing is God's goal, often our chosen route to it is wrong. So much of what we do is about *us* doing with his help, *us* achieving with his help. Satan is also master at having us believe, albeit unconsciously, that we are somehow God's answer in a situation rather than God being ours. He focuses our minds on what we can be and what we can do for him, rather than what he can be and do for us.

Samuel Brengle, probably The Salvation Army's greatest holiness teacher, battled with this very issue. He once thought, 'With the Holy Spirit, I can be a preacher.' In this way he thought he would be glorifying God. Then he saw that God could be best glorified by winning sinners. He thought, 'With the Holy Spirit I can have an appointment in a big church and so win many.' But as he prayed he saw this to be a very much self-centred desire. He then said, 'Lord if only you will sanctify me, I will take the poorest appointment there is!' His thinking was that even in the poorest of appointments he could still be a great preacher, but the Holy Spirit showed him that this was still self-centred ambition. It was still about God making him great, him being 'Something,' a 'Someone.' Finally Brengle prayed, 'Lord I wanted to be an eloquent preacher but, if by stammering and stuttering rather than eloquence I am able to bring greater glory to thee, then let me stammer and stutter.' Later Brengle said, 'I was willing to be a failure if only God would cleanse and dwell in me!'

Unable to stop our longing to please God and to reverse our commitment, Satan offers the very thing we seek, a route by which we might glorify God. But should we analyse what he offers, like Brengle we will discover that it is nothing of the sort. Satan does indeed masquerade himself as an angel of light just as Paul claims in 2 Corinthians 11:15. He makes promises, attractive promises that he cannot keep. He offers more attractive routes to God's glory, routes that do not involve a cross. But those routes will never glorify God, even if they impress man, even though they are seductive and seem a road that is more likely to succeed. As friendly as Satan may appear with his offers, and though he comes in the guise of a friend with our best interests at heart, as he did with Jesus in the wilderness (Matthew 4:1-11), and when he spoke through unsuspecting Peter (Matthew 16:22,23), he will always be seeking our ruin. He will always be trying to undermine God's will. Satan's sugar lumps are always coated in strychnine. We can never do business with the Father of Lies. The desirable ends never justify the means.

Neville Chamberlain, Britain's Prime Minister, signed the Munich Agreement on September 30th 1938, where transfer of the Sudetenland from Czechoslovakia to Germany was agreed without Czechoslovakia's involvement. Adolf Hitler assured the delegates who signed it that there would be no further territorial claims on Czechoslovakia. Hitler also agreed to a collective agreement guaranteeing the borders between Czechoslovakia and Germany. After some rest Chamberlain went back to Hitler and asked him to sign a peace treaty between Germany and Great Britain. After Hitler's interpreter translated it for him, Hitler happily signed it. Chamberlain returned to Britain to the adulation of the crowds, holding the agreement aloft for all to see. The royal family and many politicians congratulated him. Some enthusiasts felt he ought to be nominated for the Nobel Peace Prize. Others thought he ought to be rewarded with a knighthood. When earlier he boarded his plane to Germany he had told a reporter, 'My objective is peace in Europe,' and returning to London he thought he had achieved it. But one can never do a deal with the devil. Nothing is ever as Satan would make it appear. The following March Hitler invaded the rest of Czechoslovakia.

We were appointed to a corps whose twenty-five year old building was in need of improvements and an extension. Three years on, after much prayer, I shared proposals with the leadership team. They agreed with what was suggested. The question then arose as to how it would be paid for. Back then £36,000 was an even greater amount of money than it is today so the question was not an unreasonable one. We had no capital set aside and until recently the corps had depended on a subsidy from headquarters to pay its way. Although we were now self-sufficient financially, there was no surplus income. Whilst praying about the whole issue I had come to the conclusion that God didn't want us to do any money-raising, but that in this instance we were to pray for him to provide what we needed. I concluded that if the vision was from him he would also know where the means to fulfill his vision would come from.

Now, as you will already have read, I am not against fundraising, but I was convinced we were not to divert our energies in that direction. However, the path we were about to set out on was not a path I had trodden before and, in leading the people in this direction, I wanted to be sure that it was of God. Perhaps it is me and my spiritual shallowness, but I am rarely absolutely sure of anything! I always doubt whether I have got it right, whether my spiritual antennae is tuned into what the Lord is actually saying. So, despite my uncertainties and doubts, I presented what I felt the Lord was wanting to my leaders and, you've guessed it, the group was divided in their response. It didn't help when one of them asked, 'Are you sure?' and I had to answer that I wasn't without doubts. Although the leaders were equally divided about what we should do, there was actually one more person in favour of moving forward in faith with the project than those against doing so. Consequently, we decided to go ahead.

There followed a minor miracle. Over each of the next three months we had £1,000 of extra income, mainly from donations from outside the corps. In my excitement at what I saw as the Lord's provision, I mentioned to my treasurer how thrilled I was at what God was doing in answer to prayer, and how the work would be paid for in less than three years. My treasurer responded by saying that he wasn't sure about that, but that in all his years as treasurer he had never seen money coming into the corps as it was doing. However, having confidently expressed what I thought God was doing, almost immediately there was a cessation in this surplus money coming in and, over the next few months, we struggled to pay the bills. I was dismayed at this turn of events. I praised the Lord for what he had already supplied and prayed expectantly for him to continue that provision.

As time went on, I got more and more anxious. I had proudly announced to the whole corps what God was doing, predicting that a large portion of what was needed would be in place before ever the work started. Now, as one week followed another, I had nothing to announce. I was embarrassed. I feared people asking questions to which I didn't have an answer. It seemed that my pleas to God were going unheeded. What was I to do? It wasn't just a case of acquiring the needed funds. Many of our people were now expecting God to supply our needs. The faith of many of them had increased on the basis of the information I had given them since the decision to go ahead had been made. I didn't want them to be disappointed with God. I wanted them to believe that the God of the Bible was just the same today; that he can do the miraculous things today that he did in the past; that he is still the same Jehovah-Jireh (Genesis 22:14), the great Provider; that he can supply all our needs. Such motives, aspirations, desires, may well be good and pure, but perhaps, hidden under the surface was also my concern over wanting to save face and a fear of having got it wrong, fear of appearing a fool, losing credibility.

The thought then popped into my head. 'Why not try and resolve the situation?' Rolls Royce, the manufacturer of luxury cars had a factory in our town and were doing very well with very full order books. One of our people worked there and had arranged for me to have a guided tour of the works. I knew that the corps had never appealed to them for financial help before and, knowing the good work we were doing for the people of the town, I was fairly certain they might well give generous consideration to any request we might make to them. In any other set of circumstances it would not have been an unreasonable thing to do. The problem was that I had stated to our people that I felt convicted that God wanted us to pray and leave the providing to him. The temptation was to help him do what he didn't seem to be doing!

In doing so, I could argue that I did not want the faith of those who were now beginning to believe in God's ability to provide without any human assistance, to be jeopardised. I could also argue that I needed to prevent those who thought we were wrong at even considering such a perilous course of action, those who didn't believe in man ever suspending his rational thinking in response to God's directing, having a field day. And what if I had got it all wrong, and God did not ordain the course of action we had set out upon? What if the doubts I had at the beginning all turned out to be justified?

As I pondered it all, what became clear to me was that to go down the course of action that had entered my head and offered itself to me, would involve deceit. I would need to pretend that Rolls Royce had offered a donation to me, rather than that I had requested one from them. That would result in me having to claim that the Holy Spirit must have directed them. Now I know that the Holy Spirit does direct non-believers to do things, even though they do not recognise their inclination to have come from him, but that would not have been the case in this instance. So, despite the temptation, I did nothing. I waited. There were those within the corps who offered to raise money. Their motives were good, they meant well. It was hard to turn their kindness down, but I did. After much prayer and internal agony, and what seemed a very long time, out of the blue we received notification of over £5,000 being left to the corps in the form of two small legacies. I was so relieved. It had been a truly testing time.

Following that welcome news, income exceeding our expenditure started to flow again. Even though I saw a pattern emerge, I never tried to predict exactly what or how the Lord would provide for our needs again. Sadly, we were moved to another appointment before the work commenced, but in those nine months following the decision to go ahead the Lord had provided the corps with over £11,000. As we surveyed the completed work some years later, when we were invited to conduct a weekend's meetings, I was reminded again of my inner battles and how foolish I had been at giving any serious consideration to trying to do God's job for him!

In a Bible study, the subject of loving our enemies as Jesus commanded (Matthew 5:44) was being discussed. Several people commented on the natural response we have to those who would do us harm, those who hate us, which is to hurt them, harm them, display our anger to them, and let them know what they have put us through. Loving our enemies, which is far more than just tolerating them and doing them no harm, is not something that comes naturally. Jesus does not just require a passive response to their unkindness and hostility, but a positive one, 'Bless those who curse you, pray for those who ill-treat you,' he says (Luke 6:27). Someone in the group then spoke of a neighbour who she didn't get on with, someone who was very rude and unpleasant despite the fact that she had never done anything to provoke it. She found it hard not to exchange venom for venom, unkindness for unkindness, but knew that, being a Christian, she was not to. But her grace and pleasantness towards her adversary had no effect on the woman's behaviour at all. The idea of her then bestowing blessing on her 'enemy' seemed in the circumstances ridiculous, an impossibility.

Then one day whilst reading her Bible, she came to Romans 12:20, 'If your enemy is hungry, feed him; if he is thirsty, give him something to drink. In doing this you will heap burning coals on his head.' 'Ahhh,' she thought to herself, 'I'll make you feel bad. I'll heap burning coals on your head, that's what I'll do.' So she baked a cake and took it to the woman. The woman declined to come to the door and told her to go away. Annoyed at the woman's response and her unwillingness to open her door, she nearly walked away with the cake but, thinking better of it, she left it on the doorstep. A few hours later there was a knock on her door and there stood her 'enemy' somewhat emotional, full of gratitude towards her.

'I felt awful,' the lady told the Bible study group. 'As I looked at my neighbour standing before me, near to tears, I realised that whilst I obeyed quite literally what St Paul said in that verse, and gave food to my enemy, I did it to shame her with my goodness, to make her feel uncomfortable. I didn't do it out of love for the lady.' She had discovered that her obedience to God was only partial. Her motives were wrong. Doing good to those who do us harm may well result in them having burning coals on their heads, but that should not be the reason we do what we do. That motivation is to wish them hurt and harm as readily as punching them or speaking spitefully to them. As the lady quite honestly stated, she did not do what she did out of love for her neighbour. However, God graciously overrides our faults and failures sometimes. He did so on this occasion. Despite wrong motives there was reconciliation between the two and they are now friends. And the Lord taught her something more about the subtleties of Satan. A hidden danger in an instance such as this, when everything works out in the way we hoped it would, is that we can foolishly think we did the right thing in the right way when we didn't.

I do not want to spend any more time examining the deviousness and deceptiveness of Satan. He tries to take advantage of every situation. He knows our weaknesses, our foibles. He knows exactly which buttons to press. When he cannot lure us into obviously wicked ways, he will offer us good things. The fruit on that tree that our first parents were forbidden to eat wasn't poisonous, it was 'good for food' (Genesis 3:6). He will offer us things that will help us achieve God's goals, or so it would appear. The Jews were looking for a mighty military leader to conquer their foes and establish God's kingdom. They expected God to establish his kingdom by force and with strength. But he came in weakness. An end that God desires must only ever be achieved by God's means. Only by going God's way will he be glorified, and his glory is the only reason for us doing anything.

CHAPTER 23

THE SPLENDID DISCOVERY

For some reason God always seems to choose the most unlikely course of action. As Justin Welby, Archbishop of Canterbury stated in his sermon at his enthronement in Canterbury Cathedral, 'The utterly absurd is completely reasonable when Jesus is the one who is calling.'

Brengle thought more could be achieved for God if he was high and lifted up. Many Christians make the same mistake. They think, 'If only I was in that position,' or 'If only I had their gifting,' there's no telling what I could achieve for the Lord. Often they try to mimic others, model their lives on other Christians they admire and consider successful. When it doesn't work they feel discouraged and often it results in unintended jealousy. In Jesus we see God operating in the opposite direction to the one that we would expect to bring success. And he would have us follow Jesus in that direction and discover not what we might achieve for him but rather, what he is able to do for us. Dying does not appear to be the way to achieve anything. There is definitely nothing attractive about it. There is no greater weakness than that found in death. There is no greater example of faith and dependency upon God, than when Jesus willingly died and was laid lifeless in the tomb.

What the Lord requires of those who belong to him runs counter to our human nature, our natural inclinations and our understanding. No wonder we read in Proverbs 3:6, 'Trust in the Lord with all your heart and lean not on your own understanding.' God gave us a brain, we have accumulated knowledge and experience, but God desires that we do not lean or rely on it. God will so often defy what we consider to be logical or rational and require the seemingly absurd. We see that principle in action when Jesus beckoned Peter to get out of the boat and walk on the water towards him, with the simple words, 'Come.'

Our problem in following Jesus and the way of the cross is that we allow the 'what ifs?' to get the better of us, just as Peter did when he looked away from Jesus and turned his attention to the wind and the waves. We can imagine him suddenly thinking to himself, 'What on earth am I doing?' We find it so difficult not to want to maintain some sort of control, something solid to hold on to. Fear holds us back as it did on another occasion when Peter denied even knowing Jesus. He could see where it might have led, had he identified himself with Christ. Who wants to die? Who wants to be crucified?

Yet, as I looked back over those three years in North Wales I could see that before I ever really considered my need to die and what it meant to die; before I gave any in-depth thought to the subject, the Holy Spirit was showing me what he himself could do in the absence of me taking the initiative. On those occasions where he obviously prompted me to do things and say things that, had I given them more consideration, I may well have dismissed as ridiculous, I discovered how wonderfully he made everything fit together. Sometimes I was overwhelmed with the unexpected outcome and the detail of what God put in place. But those experiences were spasmodic. More often than not, though I prayed about everything, my prayers were more about him helping me than him enabling or empowering me to see and tune into the part he wanted me to play in what *he* was doing.

Inadvertently, as I have said previously, I thought the Christian life was all about me doing my very best for God, and seeking his inspiration and help to achieve it. Is it little wonder that when I sought the Holy Spirit's help in this way it rarely seemed forthcoming? However, as I look back and examine both the events reported in this book and other incidents not recorded, I realise that it was on those occasions when I didn't know what to do or how to react, or when I managed not to respond to something in the way I felt inclined to do, that something quite remarkable happened. God himself did things. In many ways it was not unlike our salvation. Only when we realised that we were not as good as we thought we were and were not all that we would have others believe and we humbled ourselves before God, accepting ourselves as sinners in need of a Saviour, a rescuer, was God through Jesus able to intervene and rescue us.

As I reviewed the experiences of the past in the light of scripture, it dawned on me that the life that Jesus died to give us, the abundant life, the life pleasing to God, a Christlike life, was not something I could ever achieve through all my efforts and energies. From bitter experience I discovered that such a course almost inevitably would end in failure and misery. Should there be a modicum of what I judged to be success, it would often result in me being proud of what *I* had done. Also, everything was all such a struggle. I was always trying hard and never quite getting it right. I dared not relax for a moment for fear that I might make a slip through lack of concentration. Always, whether it be in word or action or thought or motive, there would be a flaw. Nothing on my part was ever pure and unadulterated goodness.

St Paul knew that struggle. 'When I want to do good, evil is right there with me. For in my inner being I delight in God's law; but

I see another law at work in the members of my body, waging war against the law of my mind and making me a prisoner of the law of sin at work within my members. What a wretched man I am! Who will rescue me from this body of death?' (Romans 7:21-24).

When Jesus died on the cross he was given a criminal record. In fact he had the worst criminal record in history. Every sin, every contravention of God's law from the first sin until the end of time was recorded on his account as though he had committed them all. Thus, the curse of God on humanity came down in all its enormous weight and severity upon him, that one single, suffering, innocent man. Our slates were washed clean. There is now no trace that we ever did anything unrighteous. What a glorious and costly gift God gave us through the shed blood of Jesus.

But more than that. We need more than forgiveness for the sins we have committed and will commit. We need to be delivered from the power of sin, Satan's power over us, or 'this body of death' as Paul called it (Romans 7:24). The cross of Christ dealt with that too, 'Thanks be to God – through Jesus Christ our Lord!' said Paul (v. 25). We were trapped like slaves. 'I tell you the truth, everyone who sins is a slave to sin,' Jesus said (John 8:24). When Jesus was nailed to the cross so were we. 'We are convinced that one died for all, therefore all died' (2 Corinthians 5:14). We were united with him in his death. In fact Paul reminds the Romans in 6:6, that it is something they already know, 'For we know that our old self was crucified with him so that the body of sin might be done away with, that we should no longer be slaves of sin – because everyone who has died has been freed from sin.' We are one with Christ. When he died, we died. Paul calls us to accept this as fact and to live according to that fact. '... count yourself, (v. 11), look upon yourself, (JB Philips), reckon yourself (AV) dead to sin, but alive to God in Christ Jesus.'

My mother and father acquired their first television towards the end of the 1950s. It was a black and white receiver and took several minutes to warm up. Sometimes we lost the sound. Other times there would be interference or picture distortion, but my two brothers and I loved it. Every night there seemed to be different cowboy and indian adventure screened. Our parents ensured that we got on with our school homework by making its completion a condition of us watching these westerns. One result of this constant diet was that we would re-enact the battles we had watched with our friends on the council estate, with half of us cowboys and the other half Indians. If someone on the opposing side 'shot' you with their toy gun you were meant to lie down 'dead.' You were out of the game. But as you can imagine, there were often disputes. 'You missed!' 'I shot you first!' Sometimes someone 'killed' at the beginning of rather a long game would get up and join in again until they were spotted and harangued by the enemy, 'You're dead. What are you doing running about?' Though 'dead' the child did not count themselves dead, did not reckon themselves dead.

When we accepted the fact that all those centuries ago Jesus died on the cross and that his shed blood washed away all our sins, we then lived as though it were true. Satan might taunt us and plant thoughts in our minds suggesting that it is all an illusion; we might on occasions wonder how someone like us could be forgiven; we might not feel forgiven. But none of this alters the fact that we were, that we are. God would have us live continually in the assurance of his word, 'that whosoever believes in him shall not perish but have eternal life' (John 3:16) and 'If we confess our sins, he is faithful and just and will forgive our sins and purify us from all unrighteousness' (1 John 1:10). He would have us take him at his word and live accordingly. That is what faith is. And when we do that God fulfils other promises that confirm that God is faithful to his word.

In Romans 6:6 Paul reminded his readers that they have been crucified with Christ, and in verse 11 he is saying, 'now live accordingly, *count yourselves dead*, don't go on behaving as though it isn't true.' Paul exhorted the Colossians on the same point, 'Since, then, you have been raised with Christ, set your hearts on things above, where

217

Christ is seated at the right hand of God. Set your mind on things above, not on earthly things. For you died, and your life is now hidden with Christ in God' (Colossians 3:1-3). In other words, 'become what you are.'

When it comes to dying, there is an absolute breach between death and life. The two cannot be reconciled. When someone is dead they are no longer affected by the things that affected them before. They are no longer controlled and influenced by what held sway in their lives before. Sin has no control over a dead person. A dead person is freed from its enslaving power. In death Jesus was separated from all that surrounded him. He ceased to see or hear anything. He was totally unaffected by what was around him.

'I have been crucified with Christ,' Paul said (Galatians 2:20). Later, he states, 'Those who belong to Christ Jesus have crucified the sinful nature with its passions and desires' (Galatians 5:24). There was only one way that Christ could experience the resurrection life and share it with you and me, and that was by first dying. It is in accepting and sharing his death that we can share in his resurrection life (Romans 6:5). When we count ourselves dead (v. 11), reckon ourselves dead, (AV), what liberation we find. The hole left behind with the departure of 'the old man' is filled with something far more wonderful by the 'new man.' No longer are we struggling to be like Jesus. We no longer need to put all that effort in. It was a lost cause. Only Jesus could ever be like Jesus. We could never please God however much we tried. But with ourselves dead and out of the way, Jesus is able to live his life in our place.

As Paul says, 'I no longer live, but Christ lives in me.' Our new life is a daily identification with Christ, consisting of sharing both his death and his resurrection. 'We always carry around in our body the death of Jesus, so that the life of Jesus may also be revealed in our body. For we who are alive are always being given over to death for Jesus' sake, so that his life may be revealed in our mortal body' (2 Corinthians 4:10,11). Again, I repeat 1 Corinthians 15:31

where St Paul states, 'I die every day – I mean that, brothers – just as surely as I glory over you in Christ Jesus our Lord.'

There is a closeness with Christ, a deep and abiding fellowship that is only to be found in our dying with him, dying to self as he died to self. 'I want to know Christ,' said St Paul, 'and the power of his resurrection and the fellowship of sharing in his sufferings, becoming like him in his death, and so, somehow, to attain the resurrection from the dead' (Philippians 3:10). To Paul, everything else was rubbish compared to 'the surpassing greatness of knowing Christ Jesus my Lord' (v. 8). That which the world values, and at one time Paul valued too, he now considered of no worth or consequence' (v. 7). When we accept that the 'old man' has been crucified with Christ, the new creation that is resurrected in his place sees everything differently and values everything differently. Christ is in us and we in him. All that we require to live a fruitful life, pleasing to God, is to remain in him and him in us. As Jesus himself said, 'Remain in me ....' He lets us control our surrenderedness. 'Remain in me, and I will remain in you. No branch can bear fruit by itself; it must remain in the vine. Neither can you bear fruit unless you remain in me' (John 15:4). 'If a man remains in me and I in him, he will bear much fruit; apart from me you can do nothing' (v. 5).

Much that is done in Christ's name is carnal and is measured from a carnal rather than a spiritual perspective. So much is the 'old man' at work, 'the 'old man' full of good intentions. Whatever our good intentions, unless our life is a daily identification with Christ in his death and resurrection, what we do will not be done by the Christ in us, but rather that 'old man,' and we will not look at the issues through his eyes for we will not have the new man's eyes. What we may look on as gain, as achievement, even if it receives acclaim from Christian friends and congratulations from the world, will ultimately achieve nothing of any real consequence. The reason is that with all our praying and requests for God's blessing upon it, it will not have been the Christ in us from whence it came ... 'apart from me you can do nothing' (v. 5). Also, the reason that often we do not experience the resurrection life is because we set limits on what can and cannot be crucified, destroyed, put to death. We, just like King Saul, keep things back that we value, things that we feel can be devoted to God's service and then organise what we do around these things.

In addition, we cannot dictate what we are to do for him. We cannot consecrate ourselves to a particular Christian work of our choosing or according to what we believe to be our gifting. Our consecration has to be to the will of God, to be and to do whatever he requires. That will result in a daily, moment by moment seeking after him and what he desires, rather than slotting ourselves into a role of Christian service that merely requires us to fulfil a job description. Our problem as ever is our wills. As Watchman Nee says, 'That strong self-assertive will of mine must go to the cross, and I must give myself wholly to the Lord. We cannot expect a tailor to make us a coat if we do not give him any cloth, nor a builder to build us a house if we let him have no building material; and in just the same way we cannot expect the Lord to live out his life in us if we do not give him our lives in which to live. Without reservations, without controversy, we must give ourselves to him to do as he pleases with us.'

Those who so trust in the Lord that way, can rely on his providential care and protection like King David:

> *'The Lord is my rock, my fortress and my deliverer;*
> *my God is my rock, in whom I take refuge,*
> *my shield and the horn of my salvation.*
> *He is my stronghold, my refuge and my savior;*
> *from violent men you save me.'*
> 2 Samuel 22:2-3

With that knowledge and assurance we know that nothing can hurt or harm us without the Lord's permission or say so. When we look at the life of Jesus we see him being saved from his enemies on many an occasion. He was saved from Herod's murderous plan when he was an infant (Matthew 2:13-16), from being thrown off a cliff in Nazareth (Luke 4:29), and from being stoned in Jerusalem (8:59). But the day came when God allowed men's hate to reach him and nail him to a cross. The same happened to Paul. We read in Acts of the Apostles a number of accounts of him escaping death, but the time came when the Lord allowed him to be taken to Rome and put to death.

The fact is that when we belong to Jesus there is always a purpose behind the injustices, those unpleasant experiences and even the physical things we might suffer. We no longer belong to ourselves. We belong to Jesus. We don't have an agenda of our own, plans for ourselves. We place ourselves at Christ's disposal. We allow him to do whatever he desires to achieve his ends, whatever that might mean for us, whether it is pleasant or unpalatable, sweet or bitter. His ends are our ends.

Sometimes we struggle to be strong, to be seen as capable, knowledgeable, clever even, when often God would use our frailties, failings and feebleness if only we would let him. He would reveal his strength amid our weakness if only we were prepared to accept our weaknesses instead of disguising or denying them. Frequently, it is only after we have exhausted ourselves in trying to succeed and been found wanting, that we collapse in a heap at his feet and plead for him to do something. Often the Lord can only get on with doing what he wants to do when we have given up trying to do it for him.

In an earlier chapter I spoke of my helplessness in the hopeless situation we found ourselves in when we arrived at our second appointment, and the tears I shed before the Lord as I sat on that smelly sofa. Although it was many months before I actually saw any evidence, God responded to the cries of my wife and I. Gradually things started to happen. The giving of God's people increased, new people came to worship, people grew in their faith and expectation, and people got saved. Five years on, we left a very different corps than the one we had entered, very much aware that it was something that God himself had done. Incidentally, the icing on the cake was that after three years treatment our son was given the all-clear regarding his leukaemia. Today he remains healthy with no need of even an occasional hospital check-up, for which we praise God. We also thank him for the many people who faithfully prayed for him.

When we have exhausted our store of endurance,
When our strength has failed ere the day is half-done,
When we reach the end of our hoarded resources
Our Father's full giving is only begun.
Annie Johnson Flint

It isn't that we are encouraging slothfulness or idleness. The gospel certainly does not condone such things. No, there is labour to be done, but it must be done at the behest of the Christ in us, and done by Christ living his life in us and through us. 'For we are God's workmanship, created in Christ Jesus to do good works, which God prepared in advance for us to do' (Ephesians 2:10).

Before he ascended into heaven Jesus made it quite clear what he desired of his disciples. They were to be his 'witnesses in Jerusalem, and in all Judea and Samaria, and to the ends of the earth' (Acts 1:8), to 'go and make disciples of all nations' (Matthew 28:19). It was a mammoth and formidable undertaking for men who had so recently revealed themselves to be unreliable, complete failures, incapable of fulfilling the simplest of tasks. Before his arrest, Jesus requested their support in the Garden of Gethsemane several times. All he wanted was that they stay awake and pray (Matthew 26:36-45). Each time he went to them they were asleep. They had all said they would never let him down (Mark 14:31), but as soon as the soldiers came to arrest him they were off! Every man for himself!

Jesus knew that, of themselves, they were incapable of doing what he wanted. Only Christ in them could ever fulfill Christ's desires. For their part, having been so confident in themselves in the past, only to discover their ineptitude, incompetence and weakness, the disciples now knew their severe limitations too. Following the experience of Christ's passion, gone was their self-reliance, self-confidence. Consequently, I can't help wondering if some of that waiting and praying in the upper room over ten whole days was to do with them realising the need for the 'old man' in each of them to be gone. Only with 'him' gone, dead and buried, and each of those gathered in that room giving up all claims on their lives could the Holy Spirit come and fill them and give them the resurrection life Christ planned for them. At Pentecost, Jesus went from being an external physical person they all tried to follow, to someone who, by the work of the Holy Spirit, could now live within each them and make himself known to them in a far more intimate way.

Having said all that, though we have been crucified with Christ, Satan continues to try and reverse what Christ has done. He is in the resurrection business too, or tries to be. That which is dead and buried in Christ he attempts to dig up and place back on the throne. This is why our dying needs to be, as it was with St Paul, a daily thing. We need to recognise what is happening within us. Before we act or react to anything, the perennial question we need to ask ourselves is, 'Is what I am about to say or do, the 'old man' or the 'new man,' i.e. the Christ within me. The fact that we have died with Christ does not render us immune to temptation, but instead of trying to fight Satan, we recognise the 'old man' for who he is and have the 'new man' respond. 'Abide in me,' Jesus cries. The real spiritual battle isn't so much a battle against specific temptations and sins, but a battle to keep that 'old man' dead and Christ alive within us, in other words, to permanently abide in Christ. With the 'old man' dead and Christ alive and filling us, Satan and his subtlest attacks can be thwarted.

As an earlier chapter records, God taught me that I only have one real obstacle to the faith and trust that God desires for me: and that is me ... Howard Webber. I quote what I felt God saying: 'You only have one problem in life and it isn't the house or the corps or your health or your lack of resources, gifts and talents .... it's you. You are your only real problem.'

'Lord empty me of me and fill me with you, that all that exudes from me might be Jesus; that others might see you in me, rather than me ... Amen'

Miss Barrett meant me harm when she said what she said. She did not chastise me out of love. It was venom. It was meant to hurt. But I now thank God for what she did. Not because it was true, though it may well have been, but because it set me on a course that drew me closer to Christ and released me from so much that internally enslaved me. Sometimes the only way for our eyes to be opened to what God is trying to show us and make us, so as to be more fruitful for him, is by him putting us through a bad experience.

It reminded me of the horrible experiences, recorded in Genesis, that Joseph went through because of the hatred of his brothers who sold him into slavery. But as a result of what he went through he eventually found himself in a situation whereby he could save his family, God's chosen people, from starvation. When their father Jacob died, Joseph's brothers feared for their lives. They thought that the only reason he had not taken revenge on them for what they had done to him all those many years before, was out of his love for their father. But Joseph had genuinely forgiven them and revealed such magnanimity towards them, adding the wonderful words, 'You intended to harm me, but God intended it for good to accomplish what is now being done, the saving of many lives' (Genesis 50:20).

If grains of wheat must die
That they might fruitful be,
And Jesus died upon the cross
To bear good fruit for me,
How readily, my Father God,
Should I then die for thee.

But I abhor the pain,
I flinch and run away;
My actions in the testing times
Don't match the words I say.
How often I desert thee, I,
Who promised I would stay.

Lord, break this strong desire
That still prevails in me,
To want to save and keep my life,
Not share thy Calvary;
That I might know the wonder of
Thy fruitfulness in me.

ABOUT THE AUTHOR

Howard Webber, father of five grown up children and three grand-children, has been a Salvation Army officer for over thirty years. His ministry has included positions as a corps officer (church leader), an itinerant evangelist, a church planter and a writer. His first book, *Meeting Jesus: Inspiring Stories of Modern-Day Evangelism,* was awarded the *Premier Christianity* magazine's Book of the Year in 2010. In retirement, he and his wife Judy live in Bournemouth, United Kingdom.

Made in the USA
Columbia, SC
13 October 2017